MW01014166

90 Days in

Judges, Galatians, & Ephesians

EXPLORE BY THE BOOK
Judges, Galatians, & Ephesians

© The Good Book Company, 2017

Published by:
The Good Book Company

Tel (US): 866 244 2165
Tel (UK): 0333 123 0880
Email (US): info@thegoodbook.com
Email (UK): info@thegoodbook.co.uk

Websites:

North America: www.thegoodbook.com
UK: www.thegoodbook.co.uk
Australia: www.thegoodbook.com.au
New Zealand: www.thegoodbook.co.nz

Studies in Galatians and Judges:
Unless indicated, all Scripture references are taken from the HOLY BIBLE, NEW INTERNATIONAL VERSION. Copyright © 1973, 1978, 1984 International Bible Society. Used by permission.

Studies in Ephesians:
Unless indicated, all Scripture references are taken from the HOLY BIBLE, NEW INTERNATIONAL VERSION. Copyright © 2011 Biblica, Inc.™ Used by permission.

ISBN: 9781784981631

Printed in India

Design by André Parker

EXPLORE

BY THE BOOK

90 DAYS IN

Judges, Galatians, & Ephesians

with

Timothy Keller
& Richard Coekin

Contents

Introduction

"The words of the Lord are flawless, like silver purified in a crucible, like gold refined seven times." (Psalm 12 v 6)

This book is not an end in itself. It is a means of accessing the treasures of a far greater book. Its words are valuable only to the extent that they help you to enjoy the infinite value of words that are perfectly true, gloriously beautiful, and utterly wonderful—the words of the Lord.

It is a magnificent thing, in a world which is used to mistakes, to deceit, and to confusion, to be able to read flawless, pure, refined words. And that is what you do each time you open your Bible. God does not make errors in anything he says. He does not obscure the truth, by accident or by design. He does not fail to do anything he has said he will do.

That is why this devotional is an "open Bible devotional"—that is, you will need to keep your Bible open, on your lap or on your screen, as you use these studies. You'll be asked questions that bring you to examine and think hard about the text. The aim of the authors is to cause you to spend more time thinking about God's words than their words.

So, rather than seeing these devotionals as snacks, view them as meals. Set aside half an hour in your day to work through the study, and to respond to what you have seen. They are best done daily—but the most crucial thing is for you to find a pattern that is sustainable—better five studies a week for life, than seven studies a week for only a week!

Further, since every word of the Lord is flawless, we need to read every word in the Scriptures, rather than sticking to our favorite passages, or to an author's favorites. So *Explore by the Book* works, verse by verse, through whole books or large sections of the Bible. You will be moving through both famous books and not-so-popular ones, and within each book through much-used passages and less traveled parts. Expect to discover new favorite passages and memory verses that you had never read or noticed or appreciated before!

At the same time, God's word is not always easy to understand. Whether we are completely new to reading it, or have mined its riches many times, all of us still experience "huh?" moments as we struggle to grasp its meaning! So in this devotional series, some of the greatest Bible teachers in the evangelical world help you to dig up the Bible's treasures, and explain their more opaque aspects. They will show you how what you are reading fits into the great overall story of the Scriptures, and prompt you to apply what you have read to your life.

God's word is not simply pure—it is also purifying. It is the way his Spirit works in his people to challenge and change us. It is designed to move us to worship him with our lips, in our hearts, and through our lives. Each day, you will see one (or both) of these headings: *Apply*, and *Pray*. Use these sections to turn what you have read in God's word into words to speak back to God, and into ways you will change your life in response to God.

At the end of each study you'll find a journaling page, for you to record your response to what you have read, either in words or in drawings. Use these pages as you are led to—we all have different ways of making sure we remember what we have seen in the Scriptures, and of responding to those Scriptures. But here are a couple of very straightforward suggestions that you might like to try:

Before you work through the study, read the passage and record...

The Highlight: the truth about God that has most struck you.

The Query: the questions you have about what you have read (and your best attempt at answering them)

The Change: the major way you feel the Spirit is prompting you to change either your attitudes, or your actions, as a result of what you have read.

After you have done the study, record:

One sentence summing up how God has spoken to you through his word.

A short prayer in response to what you have seen.

I hope you enjoy these 90 days listening to the flawless words of the LORD. Be sure that they will excite, change, challenge and comfort you. Be praying that God would be using his word to bless you. There is literally nothing like the words of the LORD.

Carl Laferton, Editorial Director
The Good Book Company

Note: This devotional is based on the NIV1984 (Galatians, Judges) and NIV2011 (Ephesians) Bible translations, but it will also work well with the ESV translation.

Meet the Authors

TIMOTHY KELLER was educated at Gordon-Conwell Theological Seminary and Westminster Theological Seminary, and is Senior Pastor of Redeemer Presbyterian Church in Manhattan, New York City. He is the *New York Times* bestselling author of *The Reason for God, The Prodigal God,* and *Making Sense of God*. Dr. Keller is married to Kathy, and they have three children.

RICHARD COEKIN is Senior Pastor of Dundonald Church, Raynes Park, south-west London, and Director of the Co-Mission church network. He studied Law at Cambridge University, and theology at Wycliffe Hall, Oxford, and Moore College, Sydney. Richard has authored several books including *Gospel DNA, Our Father,* and *Ephesians For You*. He is married to Sian, and they have five children.

Day
I

Gospel Truth

Galatians 1 v 1-5

Paul was a church-planting missionary. After he planted a church and left a region, he continued to help the new congregations through his letters. One of these is this epistle to the Christian churches in part of modern-day Turkey, written by Paul only 15-20 years after Christ's death.

Paul and His Role

Read Galatians 1 v 1-2

How does Paul describe himself (v 1)?

What can you learn from verse 1 about what an apostle is?

Who is Paul writing to (v 2)?

Paul and His Message

Read Galatians 1 v 3-5

In verses 1-5, Paul offers us an outline of the gospel—and it's all about Jesus.

What does Paul, God's "apostle" (meaning "messenger"), tell us about Jesus in:

- *verse 1?*
- *verse 3?*
- *verse 4?*

This letter is all about the gospel. Given that Paul is writing to professing Christians in churches, why might this be a surprise?

The most obvious fact about the historical setting of this letter is often the most overlooked! In Galatians, Paul's going to explain in detail what the gospel is and how it works. And his audience of this outline of the gospel are people who already call themselves Christians.

Christians need the gospel as much as non-Christians do! Our problems in the Christian life come because we often lose or forget the gospel. And we progress in our faith only as we grasp and apply the gospel in deeper ways.

Apply

It is very common in Christian circles to assume that "the gospel" is something just for non-Christians.

When was the last time you thought hard about the gospel message, simply for your own sake?

Are there parts of your life in which you haven't thought about how the gospel should shape your attitudes or actions?

Imagine a child asked you what the Christian gospel is.

How would you outline the gospel to them?

Pray

Thank God for his gospel, and ask him to help you never to think you should move beyond it to more "advanced" doctrines.

Ask God to show you where your life needs to be changed by his gospel message.

~ Notes and Prayers ~

Day
2

New Gospel = No Gospel

Galatians 1 v 6-9

News has reached Paul about the Galatian church that has moved him deeply. And his emotions almost immediately express themselves...

Yesterday we looked at Paul's gospel about Jesus. How would you now explain the gospel message to a friend?

A Different Kind of Greeting

Read 1 Corinthians 1 v 3-4; Ephesians 1 v 3; Philippians 1 v 3-4; Colossians 1 v 4. Then read Galatians 1 v 6.

In most of his letters, Paul follows his greeting with a paragraph of thanksgiving and appreciation for the lives of the people.

Why is Galatians 1 v 6 such a shock?

Changing the Gospel

Read Galatians 1 v 6-9

What kind of gospel is produced when any change is made to the gospel (v 6-7)?

Why is this, do you think?

A group of teachers in Galatia had taught that Gentile (non-Jewish) Christians had to observe all the Jewish dietary laws and be circumcised for full acceptance and to be completely pleasing to God.

But by insisting on Christ-plus-something-else as the requirement for full acceptance by God, they were presenting a whole different way of relating to God (v 6) from the one Paul gave them (v 8).

Paul forcefully and unapologetically fought the "different gospel," because to lose your grip of the true gospel is to desert and lose Christ himself. Everything was at stake in this debate!

How do people "add to the gospel" today in ways that diminish its power?

Here are three quick examples:

- Being good gets you to God.
- You need to perform certain rituals, or dress in the right way, or have a particular view of dating, to be a Christian.
- You need to feel overwhelming love for Jesus to truly be saved.

Even if an Angel...

What is Paul's attitude toward those who distort the gospel (v 8-9)?

Paul's gospel is the true gospel (we'll see why over the next few days. So if we hear any "gospel" which doesn't agree with Paul's, we can know it's wrong (v 9)!

Describe Paul's frame of mind when he wrote this. What has caused it? Is he warranted?

Pray

Thank God for those who taught you his true gospel.

Ask God to enable you to care as much about gospel truth as Paul did. Ask him to help you recognize anything which in reality is a "different gospel."

~ Notes and Prayers ~

Day
3

How Paul Got the Gospel

Galatians 1 v 10-12

It seems that the people who had come to the Galatian Christians with a "gospel" (v 7) which challenged Paul's had been making some claims about Paul's integrity or reliability. In these verses, he begins to defend himself.

Read Galatians 1 v 10-12

Gospel Source

What kind of challenge does Paul appear to be answering in verse 11?

Why would this claim be damaging to Paul's argument that his gospel is the true one?

How did Paul receive his gospel (v 12)?

What a great encouragement to trust our lives and futures to this message!

Paul's Conversion

Read Acts 9 v 1-9

Saul (also known as Paul) was going to Damascus to take Christ's people prisoner; he ended up entering Damascus as a prisoner of Christ!

Paul's conversion is a great reminder that no one is beyond the reach of Jesus. If the Lord can turn this persecutor into a preacher, he can bring anyone to faith.

Are there people you know who you don't really think could ever become Christians?

Why not pray for them right now? And why not keep praying for them daily?

Paul's Answer

Perhaps "some people" (Galatians 1 v 7) were claiming that Paul had just got his message from "HQ" in Jerusalem, and were saying, "We've also been trained there. And we say Paul didn't give you the whole story. There's more to this gospel message than what he's said."

But Paul had been preaching his divinely-given gospel for three years before ever going to HQ (see v 15-20)!

Gospel Change

What results do you see in Galatians 1 v 10 of a gospel-changed life?

Whose approval could Paul seek (v 10)?

If we know God's approval, we don't need to fear any disapproval from people. And, as we'll see as we work through Galatians, the gospel tells us that God's complete favor and approval are already ours, through Christ.

⊙ Apply

To many of us, verse 10 will come as a challenge. We tend to think we can do both: live Christianly and enjoy popularity. Paul is quite clear that there will be many times when we will need to choose one or the other.

In which parts of your life do you most easily find yourself wanting to please people more than Christ?

To serve Christ in those areas, what needs to change?

~ Notes and Prayers ~

Day
4

Changed by God's Gospel

Galatians 1 v 13-24

Galatians 1 v 10 – 2 v 21 is often called the autobiographical section of the letter, because Paul talks here about his conversion and early Christian life. But Paul isn't just sharing his testimony for general inspiration; he's using it to defend the reliability of his gospel message.

Read Galatians 1 v 13-24

Before, During, After

As Paul talks about how he came to faith, he illustrates some aspects of what the gospel is.

When it comes to the gospel:

- *who makes us able to understand it (v 15-16)?*
- *what is it all about (v 16)?*
- *who is it for (v 16)?*

How does Paul see God's grace working in his life even before his conversion?

How do these verses show Paul being equipped for his ministry in and after his conversion?

⊙ Apply

In what ways, as you look back, can you see how God worked in your life:

- *before you were even born?*
- *before your conversion?*
- *since you've been a Christian?*

Speak to God now, thanking him for his work in your life, seen and unseen.

What the Christians Thought

In verses 11-12, Paul said his gospel was not made up, nor was it given to him by a man. His great claim is that his message came to him straight from Jesus himself.

How is Paul underlining this point:

- *in verses 18-19?*
- *in verses 21-22?*

Re-read verses 23-24. What results do you see here of a gospel-changed life?

How did the churches react to the news of Paul's conversion and ministry?

The apostles and the churches didn't meet Paul before he began preaching the gospel God had revealed to him. They didn't teach it to him, nor did they seek to change it. Paul is at pains to prove that his message is God-given (unlike the "gospel" other teachers are peddling in Galatia); and that the apostolic, gospel-centered churches recognized this and praised God for it.

Notice that in talking about his conversion and his message, Paul has made sure to point not to himself but to God, who deserves all the praise (v 24).

⊙ Apply

What guidance is there here about:

- *why to share our testimony?*
- *how to do so?*

Who could you point to the truth of the gospel by sharing your testimony with them?

~ Notes and Prayers ~

Day

5

A Gospel of Freedom?

Galatians 2 v 1-5

It must have been some meeting. Paul, who for fourteen years had been preaching his gospel message throughout the known world, was coming to Jerusalem to see the men who had lived alongside Jesus during his time on earth. Would they get on? Would their messages prove to be the same?

Read Galatians 2 v 1-5

Why Paul Went

In verse 1 we're with Paul in Jerusalem. Who did he take with him?

Who was he wanting to see (v 2)?

But Paul did not need human authorization to preach the gospel (1 v 12)!

So why did he want to set "the gospel that I preach" before these men (2 v 2)?

What had happened that prompted Paul's visit (v 4)?

This "freedom in Christ Jesus" is the freedom from having to obey God to make us fully acceptable to him, ourselves, and others. It's the freedom to say that we are more wicked than we ever dared believe, but more loved and accepted in Christ than we ever dared hope.

But these "false brothers" had taught the opposite to Paul: that the Gentiles had to be circumcised, as well as trust in Christ, to be completely acceptable to God.

It must have been a tense time for Paul. Did the Jerusalem leaders preach the same gospel of freedom as him?

Circumcision was crucial in this debate. It was part of what is often called the Old Testament "ceremonial laws"—detailed prescriptions about food, dress and so on that made one ritually "clean."

So, the Gentiles as a whole had always been "unclean," and therefore unfit for the presence of God—unless they were circumcised and adopted the entire "Mosaic code" for daily living.

What Paul Found

What nationality was Titus (v 3)?

In other words, not Jewish!

So why was it very significant that he was not required by the Jerusalem Christian leaders to take on the Jewish mark of circumcision?

Imagine Titus had had to be circumcised. How would "the truth of the gospel" (v 5) that Paul had been preaching have been lost?

⌄ Apply

Why does what God did that day matter to us today?

In what ways does the gospel give us freedom that "earn-your-salvation" religions do not?

⌃ Pray

Ask God to protect you from anyone or anything which could undermine "the freedom we have in Christ."

~ Notes and Prayers ~

Day
6

Church United

Galatians 2 v 6-10

Titus being accepted as a Christian without being circumcised (2 v 3) may seem obvious to us today, but for the early church it was massively significant. It confirmed that the gospel is about faith in Christ, not our deeds.

The question now was: how would Paul get on with the Jerusalem leaders? Would they be able to work side by side?

Read Galatians 2 v 6-10

Unity Expressed

As Paul met these church leaders, what did he remember (v 6)?

What did they realize about Paul and his work (v 6-8)?

In verses 7-10 we're seeing another massive moment for the church: there is unity among gospel proclaimers.

How is this unity expressed here?

The unity we see here was not unity at all costs, but unity around gospel truth.

Unity is a precious thing: but it should not be at truth's expense. Paul was willing to be disunited with those who preached a gospel of slavery to works, instead of the freedom that comes from faith in Jesus (v 5).

Can you think of examples where the church ignored truth to stay united?

What about where the church has agreed about the truth but allowed itself to be divided over other issues?

Plans Made

It was agreed that Paul should continue with his mission to the Gentiles, as the Jerusalem church focused on going to the Jews with God's gospel message (v 9).

What did the Jerusalem leaders ask of Paul (v 10)?

The Jewish churches were much poorer than the churches Paul was planting in wealthier, Gentile areas.

Why did that make it particularly important that these Gentile churches should remember the poor, do you think?

A sign of true Christian unity is tangible, practical support between churches.

Apply

Is your character one which tends to be divisive when it's unnecessary; or to exalt unity when it's impossible?

Make sure that you hold gospel truth as more important than either unity or division.

What are the two priorities of these Christian leaders in verses 9-10? Does your personal life reflect the importance of this?

Pray

Thank God that he saves very different characters, and gives them different tasks and callings.

Ask God to keep his people united around the truth of the gospel.

~ Notes and Prayers ~

Day
7

Justified by Faith

Galatians 2 v 11-16

Paul and Peter didn't always see eye to eye. Here we read of a really serious disagreement. But it prompts Paul to sum up his gospel as "justification by faith"; and to remind us that all of life must be thought out and lived out by Christians in line with this wonderful truth.

The Food Issue

Read Galatians 2 v 11-14

What caused Paul to oppose Peter (v 11)?

Gospel truth is no respecter of reputations!

Previously, Peter had been eating with Gentiles (v 12), showing that he considered them equals, fellow members of God's people through faith, with no need for them to keep the Jewish food laws.

Read Acts 11 v 1-18. Why had Peter originally begun "eating with Gentiles" in the first place?

What led him to stop eating with them (Galatians 2 v 12)?

What do you think Paul meant when he said that Peter was not "acting in line with the gospel" (v 14)?

Why was Peter being particularly hypocritical in his attitudes toward Gentile Christians (v 14)?

What was the effect of Peter's actions (v 13)?

The Gospel Answer

Read Galatians 2 v 15-16

Notice Paul doesn't simply say that what Peter is doing is wrong. He's focusing on whether Peter's actions are "in line with the truth of the gospel" (v 14).

How does Paul say someone is "justified" (v 16)? What does Paul rule out as a way to be justified?

Peter and Paul were both circumcised Jews who had spent their lives seeking to obey God's law.

Why is it significant that they still needed to "be justified by faith in Christ" (v 16)?

The actual word "justification" is a legal term. The opposite of "justified" is "condemned." In Christ, although we are sinners, we are not under condemnation. God accepts us despite our sin.

So, justification refers to God's unmerited favor in putting a sinner right with him. He not only pardons us of our guilt, but he treats us as righteous, as one of his pure and blameless people.

And anyone can have all this, simply through faith in Christ!

⊙ Apply

Why is justification by faith so exciting?

What "laws" is it easy to think will justify us before God, so that we stop relying only on the Lord Jesus?

~ Notes and Prayers ~

Day
8

The Difference it Makes

Galatians 2 v 17-21

What difference does knowing you are justified by faith make? In this passage Paul deals with the objection that it actually has a negative effect: and then he shows us the wonderful change that being accepted by God produces.

The Objection

Read Galatians 2 v 17-18

Verse 17 is a difficult verse...

What will, sooner or later, become clear about people who are "justified in Christ" (v 17)?

So doesn't believing I'm justified by Christ, not by keeping the law, encourage me to break the law, to sin?!

What's Paul's rather curt answer (v 17)?!

Verse 18 is another tricky sentence! It could mean, "If someone keeps on with the same lifestyle after receiving Christ, it proves they are using the gospel as an excuse to keep disobeying God and doing what they want." It's easy to see why someone who looked to the law for justification might worry that being justified without the law will remove any motivation to live for God by keeping that law.

Paul's Answer

Read Galatians 2 v 19-20

What does Paul say he's dead to now (v 19)?

So what is he now able to do (v 19)?

Where did the old Paul, who was obeying the law to try to gain justification, die (v 20)?

Paul is saying he never really lived for God when he was trying to save himself through obedience to the law. He was being very moral and good, but it was all done for Paul, not for God. Now that he is justified and accepted, Paul has a new motive for obedience that is far more wholesome and powerful. He wants simply to live for the One "who loved me and gave himself for me" (v 20).

So, Paul's answer is this: justification by God in Jesus gives a Christian a new and far stronger motive for obeying God than trying to be justified by works ever could.

A Way of Life

Read Galatians 2 v 21

Paul was saved initially by God's grace in Christ.

What does he know he must never do as he seeks to continue as a Christian?

If he could now merit justification, what would that mean about the cross? Why?

⊙ Apply

Christ will do everything for you, or nothing. You cannot combine your merit and God's grace.

So, which is it for you? Does Jesus' death mean everything or nothing to you?

Look back at Galatians 2 v 11-21. Which verse is most special to you? Take some time to memorize it now.

~ Notes and Prayers ~

Day 9

You Foolish Galatians!

Galatians 3 v 1-9

If the first two chapters of Galatians are Paul's personal defense—using his personal history to prove the message he preaches is a direct revelation from God—in chapters 3 and 4 we get Paul's theological defense of the gospel. He's outlining the essential content of the gospel message, and defending it with a variety of arguments.

The Gospel and Galatia

Read Galatians 3 v 1-5

Paul begins by reminding the Galatians how they came to Christ from paganism.

What was presented to them (v 1)?

How did they respond (v 2—think about what answer Paul expects from his question!)?

Who did they receive as a result of their response (v 2)?

That is how the Galatians had begun as Christians. But now they'd foolishly begun to think they needed to do something else to keep going as Christians.

What had they begun relying on to "attain [their] goal" (v 3)?

Paul is warning the Galatian Christians that it is easy to fall back into works-righteousness as we try to overcome sin and live the Christian life. But we need to deal with sin not through relying on "human effort," but by "believing what you heard"—the gospel.

The starting point of each day of our lives as Christians is to say to ourselves what Martin Luther, the great 16th-century Reformer, did each morning: "You are accepted." Through Jesus, whatever we do, or don't do, we are still accepted.

The Christian life begins through faith in Christ crucified alone. And it continues through faith in Christ crucified alone—which this church had forgotten!

The Gospel and Abraham

Read Galatians 3 v 6-9

What did Abraham "do" (v 6)?

What did God give Abraham on the basis of him doing this (v 6)?

Read Genesis 15 v 1-19 to see the background to Galatians 3 v 6.

This gives us a great insight into what "believing," or faith, is. It is trusting God to do what he's said he will do; knowing that he's able to do what we cannot do.

How is Abraham's saving faith a model for us (Galatians 3 v 9)?

Apply

Are you asking God's Spirit to keep you going and growing as a Christian; or are you relying on your own efforts?

Do you live and think and pray as though it is your faith which saves you, or as though it is your deeds?

~ Notes and Prayers ~

Day

10

Law's Curse, Faith's Blessing

Galatians 3 v 10-14

"I'm a good person." "I go to church and live how the Bible says." "God's pleased with how I live, so I'm fine with him."

It's so easy to think like that, consciously or subconsciously. But Paul identifies the huge problem with finding our confidence in what we do.

The Problem

Read Galatians 3 v 10-12

What does Paul say about a person who seeks to earn God's acceptance (v 10)?

What does relying on the law have to do with faith (v 12)?

The crucial word in verse 12 is "does." Observing the law perfectly would lead to acceptance of someone by God on the basis of what he or she does.

So why is this method of seeking to be justified doomed to failure (end of v 10)?

The Solution

Since the beginning of verse 10 is true, how can God credit any of us as righteous but not be unjust?

If I have disobeyed God's law, I am under God's curse, facing life now and eternally without his loving presence. God will not simply set his curse aside; and nothing I can do will remove that curse.

Read Galatians 3 v 13-14

How did God remove the curse from us (v 13)?

Why is it significant that Jesus did not simply take our curse for us, but that he became a curse for us (v 13)?

Christ was not a sinner: but on the cross he was treated legally as if he were a sinner. He became sin: and if Jesus became the sinner you are, then you have become perfect and flawless as he is.

Read 2 Corinthians 5 v 21; Romans 3 v 21-26; 1 Peter 3 v 18

How do these words, written by both Paul and Peter, add to your appreciation of Galatians 3 v 13?

The Result

What is the great achievement of Jesus buying us out of slavery, or "redeeming us" (v 14)?

What does Paul remind us in verse 14 is the way that these achievements come to us?

Pray

Father,

Thank you that you did not leave me under a curse as an imperfect lawkeeper.

Thank you that Christ Jesus became cursed instead of me, and died the death of a human under your punishment in my place.

Thank you that by faith I am acceptable to you, and have your Spirit.

Thank you for doing all this for a lawbreaker like me, Father.

Amen.

~ Notes and Prayers ~

Day
II

So What's the Point of Law?

Galatians 3 v 15-25

The relationship of a Christian to the law of God is a great practical question. The radical truth of justification by faith prompts us to ask, "Why did God give his law then?" and, "What's the point of the law today?"

Paul begins to address these tricky issues here.

Read Galatians 3 v 15-18

What is the example Paul uses (v 15)?

Once a legal deal has been made (e.g. a contract), and established (e.g. by being signed), it can't be changed: it's fixed.

What binding deal does Paul mention next (v 16)?

And these would all find fulfillment in a particular "seed" of Abraham, "who is Christ" (v 16).

So why was the law of Moses not able to set aside or add to the promises spoken to Abraham (v 17)?

What principle is laid down in verse 18a? Can salvation be by both promise and law?

The Law's Purpose: Number One

Read Galatians 3 v 19-20

What question does Paul ask in verse 19?

What is the answer he gives (v 19)?

So, one reason God gave the law through Moses was to show God's people how to live until the ultimate promise-fulfiller, Jesus Christ the "seed," came along.

What the Purpose Isn't

Read Galatians 3 v 21-22

God's law isn't a competing way to become right with God, set against God's promise. Why? Because the law was never intended to "impart life"; it was given to a sinful world, "a prisoner of sin."

Sinners can't obey God's law, so how could it ever have been an alternative means of gaining righteousness? If we think we can be righteous by keeping the law, we have completely missed the main point of the law!

The Law's Purpose: Number Two

Read Galatians 3 v 23-25

How does Paul explain that the law leads us to Christ?

The law does not oppose the promise, but supports it. The promise only comes home to us because of the work of the law. If we know God's standards and we know ourselves, we will know how far short of those perfect standards we fall.

And so it will be of huge relief also to know that we can be justified through faith in what Christ has done, rather than in anything we have done!

Pray

Thank God for showing you your sin each day through his law, so that you are able more and more to appreciate what you have in Christ.

~ Notes and Prayers ~

Day
12

Abba, Father

Galatians 3 v 26 – 4 v 7

The law and the gospel are not just stages in redemptive history, in God's plan to save sinners. They are also stages in an individual's journey toward God.

In Christ Jesus You are All...

Read Galatians 3 v 26-29

What is true of every Christian (v 26)?

What do we learn about what this means from verses 26-27?

Pause to think about the image of having "clothed yourselves with Christ."

What are the implications of the metaphor?

What is Paul saying in verse 28?

How does this flow from verse 26?

The Difference Between a Slave and an Heir

Read Galatians 4 v 1-7

After God's people received the law, but before God sent his Son (v 4), Paul describes them as being an heir but also "no different from a slave." God had promised to give them the estate; but they had not yet "grown up," and could not enjoy it. It would be theirs, but it was not yet theirs.

It is the same for each Christian. All humans are spiritual "slaves" before coming to Christ, desperately trying to live up to some standard (v 3).

Through the gospel, God makes us "come of age," because it tells us the God of grace did something to bring us into full sonship, so we could enjoy his estate...

What two things did God send his Son to accomplish (v 5)?

Many people remember the first of these, but forget the second. If God has only pardoned (or "redeemed") us, we will now have to live a life which is good enough to maintain God's favor.

But Christ didn't only remove the curse we deserved (though that in itself is amazing!) He also gave us the blessing he deserved—"the full rights of sons" (v 5). Our Father God's ongoing and eternal favor is just as secure as our pardon is.

Life as a Son

What are the privileges of sonship that Paul sets out in verses 6-7?

What has the Spirit been sent to do (v 6-7)?

"Abba" has no direct translation in English: the closest is "Dad." It's a familiar, fairly intimate way of saying "Father." It's worth just pausing here, to ponder the fact that we call God "Dad."

Apply

How will knowing the Creator as your Abba today make a difference to your:

- *prayers?*
- *joy?*
- *obedience to God?*
- *reaction to something going wrong?*

~ Notes and Prayers ~

Day
13

Don't Go Back!

Galatians 4 v 8-11

When the Galatian Christians turned *to* Christ, they turned *away* from something too. Paul is seriously concerned that they are about to turn *back*—and wants them to realize what a loss that would be to them.

Read Galatians 4 v 8-11

Then and Now

How does Paul describe the kind of religion the Greek Galatians had before they heard the gospel (v 8)?

What made the difference between then and now (v 9)?

What kind of religion are the Galatian Christians in danger of turning to (v 9)?

How is this an antidote for works-righteousness (i.e. thinking it's something we do that makes us right with God)?

Read Jeremiah 2 v 13 and Romans 1 v 25

How do these verses help us to understand what Paul is talking about here?

Thinking that keeping Bible rules, like Old Testament festivals (v 10), is what makes us right with God, is biblical legalism—and it's very common in churches today. And the shock here is that Paul is saying that thinking this way is actually "turning back" (v 9) to idolatry.

The Galatians were about to turn their own law-keeping into a "savior," and turn being religious into a god. Works-righteousness always creates idols, even if those idols are our church, or even our ministry to others!

Don't Go Back to Then!

Remember, God makes those with faith in Christ Jesus "sons of God" (3 v 26).

How does idolatry compare (end 4 v 9)?

Why do you think this made Paul fearful for them (v 11)?

⊙ Apply

Counseling expert David Powlison poses some questions to help bring idol systems to the surface. Ask them of yourself now:

- *To what do I look for life-sustaining stability, security, acceptance?*
- *What do I really want and expect [from life]?*
- *What would make me happy?*
- *Where do I look for power and success?*
- *Who or what most rules my behavior: the Lord, or an idol?*

⊙ Pray

Thank God that through faith in Jesus you are his child, with eternal life as your inheritance.

Ask God to show you where you are living (or are in danger of living) in slavery to an idol, not as his child.

~ Notes and Prayers ~

Day
14

Effects and Aims

Galatians 4 v 12-20

Are you feeling joyful? Perhaps not happy about everything, but is there an underlying joyful tune in the melody of your life? Joy is something we all want, but it often seems elusive. And joy had gone missing from this church.

Coping with Changes of Plan

Read Galatians 4 v 12-16

What does this teach us about suffering and thwarted plans?

Can you think of personal illustrations of this in your own life?

Effects of a False Gospel

What brought Paul to the Galatians (v 13)?

How had these Galatians reacted to Paul (v 14)?

How and why had this relationship between the Galatians and Paul changed (v 15-16)?

What does Paul feel has disappeared from the lives of the Galatians (v 15)?

If we know that we are loved by God unconditionally, through our faith in Jesus and his death, then we can be at peace. We can be joyful because we know that in Christ we have all we need, and that nothing we do (or don't do) can take God's favor away from us.

Our eternal future does not depend on us, but on the Lord Jesus. Paul's gospel of justification by faith alone produced then, and produces in us today, great joy.

Compare this with what a belief in works-righteousness produces. If my eternal future is in any way up to me and what I do or what I am, I will be anxious because I know I have fallen short, or arrogant because I measure myself against others who I see as less obedient than me. I may even be both—but I will not know joy!

Joy comes only from being a child of God (3 v 26), and never from being a slave to those "who are not gods" (4 v 8). It's not surprising that the Galatians had lost all their joy as they began to turn from faith in Christ to reliance on themselves and on worshiping their religious efforts!

Aims of the False Teachers

Read Galatians 4 v 17-20

What is the aim of the false teachers' ministry (v 17)? Who is it all about?

What is Paul aiming for in his ministry (v 19)?

What characteristics of healthy Christian relationships can you draw from v 19-20?

⊙ Apply

Do these things characterize your:

- *church family?*
- *small group fellowship?*
- *friendship with other individual Christians?*

If you share Paul's priorities and emotions, what will be different in your prayers for and actions toward Christians around you?

~ Notes and Prayers ~

Day
15

Grace to the Barren

Galatians 4 v 21-31

Paul has taught the Galatian Christians that they were fully children of Abraham the moment they believed in Christ (3 v 7). Now he uses the illustration of Abraham's two sons, Ishmael and Isaac, to make his point in a final, dramatic way.

Two Sons: the Difference

Read Galatians 4 v 21-28

What does it mean to be "under the law" (v 21)?

Paul's point isn't about what we are obeying: it's about what we're relying on.

Read Genesis 16 v 1-4; 18 v 10-14; 21 v 1-10

What are the differences in the births of these two sons (Galatians 4 v 23)?

What does Paul say each birth mother represents (v 24-26)?

What is the difference between the "children" of the two women?

This would have been shocking to Jewish ears. The residents of Jerusalem would have regarded Sarah as their mother, and Hagar as the mother of the Gentiles. Paul has in effect reversed things.

That's because trusting in God's law, as Jerusalem is doing, enslaves. It is Paul's Christian brothers who are "children of the promise" (v 28), because they are trusting in Christ and so are members of the true "Jerusalem" (v 26)—heaven.

The basic teaching is that the gospel not only makes absolutely anyone a child of God, but that the most proud and moral and religiously "able" are often the ones left out of God's family.

The gospel reverses the world's values.

⊙ Apply

How will this change the way you look at the members of your church?

What is the difference between a "religious" approach to God, and a Christian one?

Two Sons: the Relationship

Read Galatians 4 v 29-31

In verse 29 Paul draws another parallel between the two brothers.

What is he saying about the relationship between Ishmael and Isaac then?

What point is he making about those who trust in works-righteousness and those who trust in Christ in the first (and twenty-first) century (end of v 29)?

Why is this the case, do you think?

⊙ Apply

Why do religious people need the gospel?

How should you expect religious people to react to the gospel?

~ Notes and Prayers ~

Day 16

Firmly Free

Galatians 5 v 1-6

The thrust of the whole of Paul's last two chapters is stated in 5 v 1. It's what he wants his first readers, and his readers today, to do in response to the great gospel truths he's been proclaiming in the first four chapters.

Read Galatians 5 v 1-6

Stand Firm

What is Paul encouraging his readers to do in the two sentences of verse 1?

The Galatian Christians have been "set free."

Why would it be nonsensical for them to think they still needed to obey the law to be saved?

Paul says the outward expression of saving faith isn't being circumcised (v 6); it isn't not being circumcised either!

So what is it then (v 6)?

It's only if we know we're saved through faith in Jesus that we can truly love those around us.

Now we can serve God not for what he brings us, but for who he is. And we can serve others not for what they bring us, but simply for what we can give to them. Christ's love frees us to love others.

High Stakes

What is Paul warning the Galatian Christians about in verse 2?

As soon as we start trusting for salvation in the Lord Jesus plus something we do, we are not trusting fully in Christ; and so he is no longer our invaluable Savior. Christ plus anything means that we lose Christ.

What are the serious consequences of seeking to be justified by what we do (v 4)?

What is one area of your life where your actions will change if they are driven by love for others?

How can Galatians 5 v 5-6 help to motivate you?

Is Paul saying in verse 4 that the Galatians who are real Christians are going to lose their salvation?

Read Galatians 5 v 10. How does verse 10 shed light on verse 4?

Paul clearly believes these are real Christians who will not turn their back on the gospel. If they are Christians, who believe the gospel in their hearts, they will respond positively to his warning.

Pray

Ask God to enable you to keep knowing the priceless value of Jesus Christ, your only Savior.

Ask God to help you to stand firm in gospel freedom all your days, and to keep giving you true faith, which shows itself in real love.

~ Notes and Prayers ~

Day
17

Don't Run Off Course!

Galatians 5 v 7-12

You can almost feel the emotion and frustration pouring through Paul's pen and onto the page as he writes to these Christians who are considering throwing their faith away.

Knocked Off Course

Read Galatians 5 v 7-10

What does Paul say in verse 7 about the Galatians' performance as Christians:

- *in the past?*
- *in the present?*

What does he know has caused this change (v 7)?

Paul is picturing the Christian life as a race. And the Galatian church were fast starters. But clearly someone has cut them up, and they've been knocked off course. Now there's a chance they won't carry on in the race at all.

And that false teacher (or teachers) has done something particularly dangerous: he seems to have convinced the Galatians that his is the authentic Christian message. So Paul points out that God, "the one who calls you," would never seek to persuade his people not to obey the truth of the gospel of salvation by faith (v 8).

The false teachers were few: but what kind of effect had they had (v 9)?

Why do you think Paul includes the first sentence of verse 10? What is he encouraging the Galatians to do?

Pray

It's easy to think that this kind of thing couldn't happen to us, or to our church. But these Christians in Galatia had been "running a good race" before they were knocked off course.

Pray for yourself: that God would keep you trusting in the gospel truth, and that you would not change course for anyone or anything.

Pray for your church: that God would protect it from persuasive, all-pervasive false teaching.

Still on Course

Read Galatians 5 v 11-12

There are two "gospels" being preached:

- "circumcision": relying on what we do to make us right with God.
- "the cross": relying on what Jesus has done to make us right with God.

Which one is Paul preaching (v 11)?

How does he feel about those who are preaching the other "gospel" (v 12)?!

Paul says, *If these false teachers are so keen on chopping bits off themselves in circumcision, I wish they'd chop the whole thing off!*

Apply

What would you say to someone who says, "That church up the road which says we need to do good as well as trust in Jesus—it's fine, it's just a different type of Christianity"?

~ Notes and Prayers ~

Day
18

Our Freedom and God's Law

Galatians 5 v 13-15

At the beginning of chapter 5, Paul re-introduces the idea of Christian freedom that he mentioned earlier (2 v 4). The concept of Christian "freedom" is easy to misunderstand—and in this section Paul seeks to help us grasp what it actually means for our day-to-day lives.

How to Use Your Freedom

Read Galatians 5 v 13

What does Paul remind his readers is the status of Christians?

How could we misuse this freedom?

What error in thinking lies behind this misuse, do you think?

How should Christians use their freedom?

Freedom and the Law

Paul says we are free from the "supervision" of the law (3 v 25) and we are no longer "under" the law (5 v 18). So does that mean that we are free to disobey or disregard it? That's the question Paul is dealing with here.

Read Galatians 5 v 14

How does Paul sum up the law, and who summed it up like this before him (v 14)?

What's the relationship between freedom, love and God's law?

"You, my brothers, were called to be free" (v 13). Christians are not obliged to obey the law in order to be saved.

But now that we are saved wholly and freely by grace we are, if anything, more obligated to obey the law! Why?

Because we have more reason to love God (v 6) than ever before. Obeying the law is the way we please him—and we will gratefully want to please the One who saved us at such cost.

Freedom from Biting and Devouring

Read Galatians 5 v 15

The Galatian church was slipping back into an attitude of works-righteousness.

How were they treating each other (v 15)?

What does Paul warn them about (v 15)?

Why might we expect this to be the consequence of people relying on being good themselves, rather than on how good Christ is?

⊙ Apply

From these verses, how would you answer someone who asked you the question, "Why does a Christian obey God?"

~ Notes and Prayers ~

Day
19

Gospel Character

Galatians 5 v 16-25

In rules-based religion, the motivation for morality is rooted in fear: "I must do good things or God won't accept me." In gospel Christianity, the motivation is a dynamic of love: "God has lovingly accepted me, so I'm free to do good out of love for him and for others."

Now Paul spells out just how we grow in character through this new dynamic.

The Battle

Read Galatians 5 v 16-18

What two things are at work in every Christian (v 16-17)?

Why does this produce a conflict in us (v 17)?

What does a Christian naturally want to do?

- *verse 16*
- *verse 17b*

And so there's a great battle within us!

In verse 16 Paul talks of our "sinful nature"; in verse 18 he describes the same thing as being "under law." And this shows us how the sinful nature operates. When we look at God's law, our sinful nature sometimes uses it to encourage us to think about breaking it in some way (see Romans 7 v 7-11).

But other times, as we look at God's law, our sinful nature points out that we've kept his law, prompting in us pride and self-righteousness. That's a more subtle work of our sinful nature: a self-righteousness produced by our good works.

Being led by the Spirit frees us from this. He enables us joyfully to repent of both our sinful law-breaking and our sinful law-keeping, and so to really change.

The Victory

Read Galatians 5 v 24-26

What's happened to our sinful nature (v 24)?

It's already been defeated by God's Son at the cross! And God's Spirit applies Christ's victory there to our lives now, winning battle after battle over our defeated sinful natures.

The Product

Read Galatians 5 v 19-23

What do you learn about the human heart from the list in verses 19-21?

In what ways are the outworkings of the Spirit's work in us (v 22-23) the opposite of the sinful nature's acts?

⊙ Apply

Which of the attitudes and actions of verses 19-21 do you particularly recognize in yourself?

In which areas of your life do you need to start "keeping in step with the Spirit" (v 25)?

⊙ Pray

Ask God's Spirit to lead you in fighting your sinful nature and producing his fruit in those parts of your life.

~ Notes and Prayers ~

Day
20

Gospel Relationships

Galatians 5 v 26 – 6 v 6

This short passage is bristling with practical principles for how we relate to others.

Read Galatians 5 v 26 – 6 v 6

Provoking and Envying: How to Avoid

What does Paul warn his readers not to become (v 26)?

From 6 v 1-5, how would you define conceit?

Conceit is a desire to be given the honor and glory we feel we deserve. We want to be noticed! So we feel we need to prove our worth, to ourselves and to others. This fixates us on constantly comparing ourselves with others. When we seem better than someone else in some way, our "honor-hunger" puffs us up and elates us. When we seem to be inferior to someone else, we are devastated.

According to verse 26, what are the two possible effects of conceit on relationships?

So conceit either leads to us saying, "I've got what you don't—ha!" (which provokes) or, "You've got what I don't—unfair!" (envy).

But the gospel creates a whole new self-image. It humbles us before others, telling us we are sinners saved only by grace. But it gives us boldness before others, telling us we are loved and honored in the only eyes in the universe that really count.

So the gospel produces a boldness and a humility that do not compete, but can increase together. And we need to preach that gospel to ourselves right in the middle of situations where we're tempted to provoke or to envy, to think of ourselves as superior or inferior.

⊙ Apply

Do you have more of a tendency to "provoke" or to "envy" in relationships?

How will you use the gospel to overcome that tendency?

Restoring and Carrying: How to Practice

What principles does Paul lay down in 6 v 1?

In 5 v 14 Paul told us the law can be summarized "in a single command: 'Love your neighbor as yourself.'"

How does he tell us we can fulfill this in 6 v 2?

Verses 2 and 5 seem contradictory! But "burdens" (v 2) is not the same as "load" (v 5). Burdens are the tasks and problems that we can help others with. The word "load" refers to a kind of backpack. God has given each of us a different set of opportunities in which to obey him. These are our load—and we must each carry that pack ourselves.

⊙ Apply

How and why do Christians struggle at living out both 6 v 1 and v 2 in relationships?

What could you do practically to obey better:

- *verse 1?*
- *verse 2?*

~ Notes and Prayers ~

Day
21

Don't be Deceived!

Galatians 6 v 7-10

As Paul reaches the end of his letter, he begins a final, climactic appeal to the Galatian Christians to hold on to the truth.

Don't!

Read Galatians 6 v 7-8

What does Paul urge the Galatians not to do (v 7)?

In some ways, this is the theme of the whole of Galatians!

What farming-based principle does Paul set out (v 7)?

Whatever you sow, you will reap. If you sow tomato seeds, you won't get corn, no matter how much you want corn to grow.

And whatever you sow, you *will* reap. Though the seed may lie in the ground for a long time, it will come up. It is not the reaping that determines that there'll be a harvest, but the sowing.

There are always a consequences to our actions. It's the way God's world works, now and beyond death.

What two ways can we sow in our lives (v 8)?

What reaping results (v 8)?

⊙ Apply

How often do you look at the "field" of your life and think about what you're sowing there?

Who will you aim to please today? Your sinful nature, or the Spirit?

Do!

Read Galatians 6 v 9-10

What does Paul tell Christians to do in both verse 9 and verse 10?

What's the great motivation of doing this as we sow to please the Spirit (v 9)?

Based on your own experience, how do we "reap" from such a lifestyle?

Verse 10 is sweeping and comprehensive in its simplicity. First, it shows that the Christian life is not all about meetings or even conversions; it is about doing good to the person before me, giving him or her what is best for them.

Second, the word "doing" reminds us that we are actively to give those around us whatever love discerns is best for them; love in deed as well as in word. This starts with our family—our fellow adopted brothers and sisters in God's church. But it's not to be limited to them.

⊙ Apply

What would it look like deliberately to "do good" to all those you meet today?

⊙ Pray

Thank God for the opportunities he gives you to do good for others.

Ask him to show you how to please his Spirit today. Pray for stamina not to grow weary in doing good.

~ Notes and Prayers ~

Day

22

How to Boast Well

Galatians 6 v 11-18

For the last few lines, Paul seizes the pen from his scribe and writes with his own hand...

Bad Boasting

Read Galatians 6 v 11-13

What does verse 12 reveal about the motives of Paul's opponents?

People find it insulting to be told that they are too weak and sinful to do anything to contribute to their own salvation.

On the other hand, the world appreciates "religion" and "morality" in general. The world thinks that moral religion is a good thing for society. And Paul says that pressure to conform to the world, to be popular with and respected by it, is what is motivating the false teachers in Galatia.

What does Paul point out about those who teach salvation by good works such as circumcision (v 13)?

What do they want to be able to do (v 13)?

These men have got into religion for the fame, prestige and honor it can bring them in the world. They love to boast about their success. Their ministry is actually a form of self-salvation.

Right Boasting

Read Galatians 6 v 14-18

Paul boasts too: what does he boast about (v 14)?

At the heart of your religion is what you boast in. *What, in the end, is the reason you are in a right relationship with God?*

If it is the cross plus your good works, then it's your works that make all the difference—it's your works you're trusting in. So you'll "boast in the flesh" (v 13).

If you understand the gospel, you'll "boast" only in the cross. You find your identity, your confidence and security not in who you are or what you do, but in who Jesus is and what he did.

What effect has Christ's cross had on Paul (v 14)?

The world has no power over, and its opinion need hold no sway over, the Christian. If nothing in the world gives me my righteousness or salvation, then there is nothing in the world that I must have that therefore controls me.

How are verses 14-15 a great summary of everything Paul has been saying in this letter?

What does living by this "rule" (i.e. trusting in and living out the true gospel) bring (v 16)?

Apply

How much do you care about what the world thinks of you?

How can you "boast" about the cross, both to yourself and in front of others?

Pray

Spend some time now thanking Christ for his cross, and for the true gospel of justification by faith.

~ Notes and Prayers ~

Day
23

Looking Back

Judges 1 v 1; Joshua 1 v 1-9; Joshua 23 v 1-13

Read Judges 1 v 1

The book of Judges begins by looking back to the time of Joshua. To understand the peaks and troughs of this period of Israel's history—to appreciate the triumphs and (more often) tragedies of God's people in the time of the Judges—we need to begin, as 1 v 1 encourages us to, by looking over our shoulders.

Live by the Promises

Read Joshua 1 v 1-9

Here is the mission of the Israelites under Joshua, the man God chose to succeed Moses as Israel's leader (v 1).

What promises does God make to Joshua and the people here?

What commands does he give (v 6-9)?

Read Joshua 23 v 1-13

A "long time" has passed between chapters 1 and 23; Joshua is an old man (v 1).

What have God's people seen him do (v 3)?

What remains to be done (v 4-5)?

What must Israel not do (v 6-8)? Why not (v 12-13)?

These verses set the scene for, and provide the yardstick by which to measure, the book of Judges. The people are in the land God promised them when they were slaves in Egypt, and their enemies have been defeated. But they still need to settle the land by taking possession of it.

Live Bravely

God's call to his people (then and now) is to combine spirituality with bravery. True discipleship involves risk-taking, because true disciples rely on God to keep his promises to bless them, not on their own instincts, plans or insurance policies.

It is hard to be truly brave without faith in God. The kind of bravery that does not arise out of faith in God is adventurism, or macho heroism, or plain cruelty. It will be rooted in insecurity, or a desperation to prove oneself, or hopelessness. Only faith-based bravery will keep people from selfishness and thoughtlessness on the one hand, and cowardice and ineffectiveness on the other.

Who Israel chooses to fight, and how they respond to victory, will show whether they are truly trusting in God; whether they are really obeying the LORD.

Apply

How we choose to live shows whether we really trust God.

What risks do you take because you trust God?

Are there times you are brave out of a desire to prove yourself?

Are there times you are ineffective or risk-averse out of a desire to protect yourself?

What would you do differently in those moments if you had a faith-fueled bravery?

~ Notes and Prayers ~

Day
24

A Mixed Start

Judges 1 v 1-36

Judges 1 tracks the success, or otherwise, of nine of the twelve tribes of Israel. Will they show the brave faith that should be the hallmark of God's people?

Faithfulness...

Read Judges 1 v 1-18

In what ways are the tribes of Judah and Simeon successful?

What does God tell Israel he wants to happen in verse 2?

How is Judah: obedient? disobedient (v 3-4)?

Between the record of Judah's performance as a whole, the narrator narrows the focus to one family among Israel. Of the generation who left Egypt, Caleb and Joshua were the only two men to remain faithful; so they were the only two whom God allowed to enter the promised land (Numbers 14 v 30).

How do we see this family trusting God and taking risks to obey him in Judges 1 v 12-15:

- *Caleb?*
- *Othniel?*
- *Acsah?*

Then, in verse 16, we meet the Kenites, distant relatives of Moses.

What do they do? How does this show that they want to enjoy the blessings of being part of God's people?

This family and these foreigners show the real, radical faith Joshua had called for.

⊙ Apply

If Caleb's family were part of your church, how would their trust and obedience show itself, do you think?

...With Flaws

Read Judges 1 v 19-36

Yet what were Judah unable to do (v 19)?

Why is this strange?

Judah would have won victory even against all-powerful iron chariots. Why? Because God is with them (v 19). And yet we are told they "could not." Since God had told them that in fact they could, this must be their own verdict, based on common-sense calculations rather than risk-taking faith. So, while Othniel attacked a city in God's strength, a whole tribe concluded they couldn't do likewise in their own strength, so did nothing.

How do we see the rest of the tribes failing fully to trust and obey God (v 21-36)?

⊙ Apply

It is not our lack of strength that prevents us from enjoying God's blessings, or stops us worshiping God wholeheartedly; it is our lack of faith in his strength. When we rely on ourselves, and base our walk with God on our own calculations instead of his promises, we find ourselves making decisions like the men of Judah.

Does this describe you in any way at the moment? What would promise-trusting obedience look like for you?

~ Notes and Prayers ~

Day

25

Can't, or Won't?

Judges 2 v 1-5

Chapter 1 reads a little like a collection of Israel's press releases about their campaign. It is their spin both on their successes, and why they weren't quite as successful as we might have expected. When we are told they "could not drive out" the Canaanites (v 19, ESV), we are inclined to agree. They did their best.

So God's assessment is sudden, shocking, and confrontational...

Read Judges 2 v 1-5

Won't

What is God's verdict on Israel (v 2)?

What does God point out they shouldn't have done, that they have (v 2—see 1 v 22-26)?

What should they have done, that they haven't (2 v 2)?

Essentially, the Israelites said, *We could not.* God answers, *No—you would not.* What Israel thought of as good reasons, God says are flimsy excuses. "God is faithful; he will not let you be tempted beyond what you can bear" (1 Corinthians 10 v 13). In obeying God, there is never a real "I can't" moment.

Our Won'ts

There may be all sorts of things in our lives which we think we are unable to do, but which actually we are refusing to do.

Here are three areas where we find it easy to say "I can't" when we mean "I won't."

- Forgiveness: *I can't forgive this/him/her.*
- Truth-telling: *I can't tell them the truth. It would destroy them/wreck our relationship.*
- Temptation: *I just can't resist, even though I know it's wrong.*

What is the solution? To remember who God is—he is the God who rescues and remains faithful (v 1). Then we will obey him radically and joyfully.

⊙ Apply

Are you saying "can't" which is in fact "won't" in any of these areas?

When do you need to remember who God is and change your "won't" to "will"?

Blessing the Unblessable

What has God promised (end Judges 2 v 1)?

What does God now promise (v 3)?

What is the apparent contradiction here?

God has promised to bless his sinful people. Yet he will also judge sinners. How can he do both? Judges does not give us the answer—only the cross does. There, God poured out his judgment on his people in the person of his Son so that he could bless his people. *Read 2 Corinthians 5 v 21.*

How does Judges 2 v 4-5 show us the right response to being confronted by our "won'ts"?

⊙ Pray

Admit to God your "won'ts." Thank him for judging them at the cross. Ask him to enable you to remember who he is, so your "won'ts" change to "wills."

~ Notes and Prayers ~

Day 26

A Second Introduction

Judges 2 v 6 – 3 v 11

This section is a second introduction to the book of Judges, which is best read as "parallel" to 1 v 1 – 2 v 5. But it is not only an introduction: it is a summary of the whole book. Here, we see the cycle of Israel's spiritual experience which we will see repeatedly throughout Judges.

The Judges Cycle

Read Judges 2 v 6 – 3 v 6

Verses 8-9 of chapter 2 take us back to the same point Judges 1 began with—Joshua's death.

What happened after the people of Joshua's generation had died (2 v 10)?

Now we are introduced to the cycle we'll see repeated in Judges, over and over:

- The people rebel—forgetting the Lord and worshiping other gods.
- God is angry.
- As a result, he allows them to be oppressed by their enemies.
- In great distress, they cry out to the God they have rejected.
- In compassion, he raises up a leader, a "judge."

- The judge rescues the people, and leads them into peace, and obedience to God.
- The judge dies.

Let's notice one particular detail:

Who exactly do the people worship (v 12-13)?

The point here is that it is possible (even natural, perhaps) for humans to worship many gods at the same time. The worldview at the time—and the worldview of our time—can accept the existence of the God of the Bible, but not his exclusive sovereignty. He can be one of many—but he mustn't be the one true God. The LORD had asked the people he had rescued and blessed to worship him alone. But they worshiped him plus others.

Apply

This is a subtle temptation for professing Christians. We live in a world which offers us a vast array of alternative gods. The greatest danger, because we can hide it even from ourselves, is not atheism but asking God to co-exist in our hearts with other gods.

How can we expose any idols we are trying to worship alongside God?

Look at each area of your life (family, career, possessions, time etc). Ask:

- *Am I willing to do whatever God SAYS about this area?*
- *Am I willing to accept whatever God SENDS in this area?*

If either answer is "no," that is an area of your life and heart you have opened to, or given to, an alternative god.

The First Judge

Read Judges 3 v 7-11

How do we see the "Judges cycle" here?

Can you think of ways that Othniel is like Jesus? What are the key differences between them?

~ Notes and Prayers ~

Day 27

The God of Left-Handers

Judges 3 v 11-31

The history of Othniel shows us the "Judges cycle" at its simplest. It is almost a template; and, as we'll see, the ways in which future cycles differ from it are important, and instructive. So it's worth setting out those stages again...

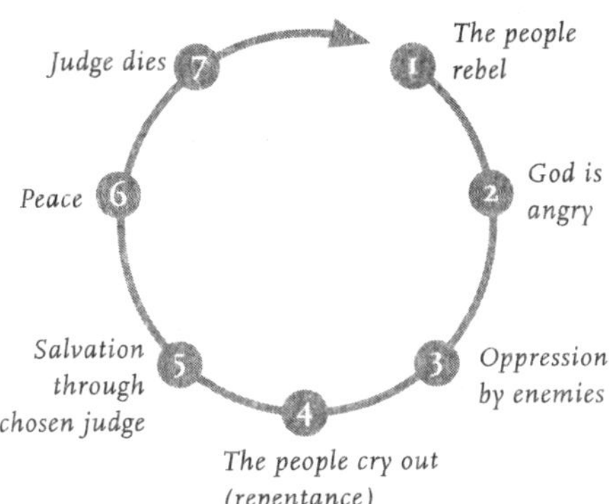

An Unexpected Judge

Read Judges 3 v 11-31

Pick out the stages of the cycle in verses 12-30.

Why was Othniel an unsurprising judge for God to choose (see 1 v 12-13)?

Why is Ehud an unexpected judge (3 v 15)?

In the Bible, references to the right hand are all positive (Isaiah 62 v 8-9; Psalm 16 v 11; 110 v 1). The right hand was a symbol of power and ability; you fought with your right hand, hanging your sword on your left thigh to make it easy to draw. And Judges 3 v 15, in the original Hebrew, suggests that Ehud's right hand was paralyzed in some way. No one would have chosen Ehud to lead—except God.

But why is it Ehud's left-handedness that enables him to defeat God's enemy (v 16-23)?

Here is an unexpected rescuer, achieving the rescue in a manner we might not have predicted. And, unlike Othniel, who "went to war," apparently with all of Israel at his back (v 10), this judge has to begin his work of rescue alone, before the people join him (v 27-29).

The Gospel for Left-Handers

Read Isaiah 53 v 2-6

How does Ehud provide us with a shadow of the Lord Jesus?

Of course, Jesus is an even more unlikely Deliverer. While Ehud delivered Israel through military triumph, Jesus rescued us by being crushingly defeated. Jesus is, supremely, a "left-handed" Deliverer.

Read 1 Corinthians 1 v 26-31

Who else is "left-handed," in the world's eyes (v 26-27)?

Why does God choose people on the margins of society (v 29)?

Apply

How is it humbling to know that God chooses "left-handers"—us?

How is it exciting to know God uses "left-handed" people like us?

Pray

Lord Jesus,

Nothing in my hand I bring,

Simply to thy cross I cling.

Amen.

~ Notes and Prayers ~

Day
28

How to Live by Faith

Judges 4 v 1-16

"The Israelites again did evil in the eyes of the LORD" (4 v 1). And so the scene is set for another judge—and another surprise.

Godly Rule

Read Judges 4 v 1-7

"Iron chariots" (v 3) were the smartbombs and drones of the age.

How is this oppression the worst yet (v 1-3)?

Who is the leader/judge of Israel in this cycle (v 4)?

Why would that have been unexpected in the ancient world, do you think?

What does Deborah do (v 5)?

Of all the judges, Deborah is the greatest pointer to the monarchy; to effective, godly, just rule. And she is a great pointer to Jesus, our "Wonderful Counselor ... Prince of Peace" who is "establishing and upholding [his kingdom] with justice and righteousness ... for ever" (Isaiah 9 v 6-7).

Here in the heart of Judges, a book of great battles, we're reminded that God's people do not only need a mighty Rescuer; we need a wise Ruler, too.

What happens if we try to treat Jesus as our Rescuer, but not our Ruler?

What about if we see him as our Ruler, but not our Rescuer?

Godly Faith

Read Judges 4 v 8-16

Through Deborah the prophetess, God calls Barak to rescue his people by defeating their enemies (v 6-7). Barak's response in verse 8 can be read in two ways. The pessimistic one is that he is being faithless, refusing to obey God unless Deborah holds his hand. The NIV1984's translation of verse 9— "Because of the way you are going about this, the honor will not be yours"—strengthens this view.

But verse 9 can also be translated as a simple statement (see NIV1984 footnote): "On the expedition you are undertaking, the honor will not be yours." This is more optimistic; Deborah is not rebuking Barak, but telling him he must charge at 900 iron chariots, and won't get any glory for it! On this reading, which I favor, Barak is a great example of real faith (as Hebrews 11 v 32-34 describes him).

How does Barak show faith in:

- *Judges 4 v 8 (remember, Deborah is the way God speaks)?*
- *verses 14-16?*

Barak does all this knowing he will not be honored for it. Real faith is concerned to obey God, not to seek praise.

Apply

Listening to God's word; obeying in trust; not seeking honor for ourselves.

In which areas of your life is God helping you to live like this?

How, and why, does this picture of real faith challenge you?

~ Notes and Prayers ~

Day 29

Death by Tent Peg

Judges 4 v 17-24; 5 v 24-31

God has told Barak that he "will hand Sisera over to a woman" (4 v 9). Presumably, to Judge Deborah? No—there's a twist in this tale...

The End of Sisera

Read Judges 4 v 17-24

Why does Sisera flee to Jael's tent (v 17)?

And, until the end of verse 20, it seems a wise decision... but it certainly isn't (v 21). Pitching tents was a woman's job, and so a tent peg was a essentially a traditional woman's household appliance, like an iron or a vacuum cleaner.

How does this make the manner of Sisera's death all the more humiliating?

How do you feel about Jael's actions? Should they be praised, criticized, or both?

Read Judges 5 v 24-31

How is Jael described in this song, sung by Deborah and Barak (v 24)?

What do we learn about how Sisera liked to enjoy his victories (v 30)?

The translation in verse 30 of "girl" is unhelpful; the ESV says, "A womb or two for every man." Sisera liked to take his enemies' women as sex-slaves for him and his men. And so his mother assumes his delayed return is because he is attacking women (v 28-30); in fact, the delay is because of a woman's attack on him.

How do you now feel about Jael's actions?

Vengeance or Forgiveness?

Through Deborah, God says Jael is honored (4 v 9) and blessed (5 v 24). Yet she has broken her culture's strict hospitality code; and she has lied and killed in cold blood. How can any of this square with Jesus' command to love, bless and pray for our enemies (Luke 6 v 27-28)?! We are right to feel conflicted or confused!

How do these New Testament passages help?

- *Revelation 11 v 15-18*
- *Romans 12 v 19-20*

How can we be sure that God "repays"? Because, on the cross, we have seen him judging sin. The cross is not only the place where we are forgiven; it is the proof that God does judge. And how do we know that God will repay? Because, in his resurrection, Jesus has been appointed as that future judge (Acts 17 v 31).

The death and resurrection fundamentally change our attitude toward our enemies. We want to see justice done, and we know that it will be, and we praise God that it will be. But we are free to love and bless and pray for our enemies. Because of the cross, we can have the attitude Jesus had on the cross, as he looked at those who were killing him and said, "Father, forgive them" (Luke 23 v 34).

⊙ Apply

Is there anyone you are judging yourself, instead of leaving it up to God?

Will you forgive them and seek to bless them? How?

~ Notes and Prayers ~

Day

30

A Different Perspective

Judges 5 v 1-31

By the end of chapter four, Jabin, the Canaanite king, is "destroyed." We should expect to read of the last stage in the cycle—peace. And we will, but not until 5 v 31. First, we are presented with the same events, from a different angle.

Read Judges 5 v 1-31

The Differences

What are the differences between Judges 4 and 5:

- *in style?*
- *in tone?*

Did you notice any different, or additional, details as you read through?

The foundational difference between the two chapters is that the approach of chapter 5 is more theological. It looks beneath the surface of history and reveals that God's hand was behind it all.

The Lord

What picture of the Lord do we get in 5 v 4-5?

Why did "the kings of Canaan" meet defeat, not victory, in the battle (v 19-22)?

On a surface level, the victory was Barak's (4 v 14-15). But even in chapter 4, we're told "the LORD routed Sisera." In chapter 5, we discover how he did it; and Barak is not even mentioned as fighting!

What lesson do you think God's people are meant to learn from this?

The LORD's people

Re-read Judges 5 v 13-18

Who fought with Deborah and Barak?

Who stayed at home?

Why are Zebulun and Naphtali singled out for particular praise (v 18)?

What is the lesson? God wins—so blessing is to be found in fighting for and with him, putting ourselves in his service.

Keeping Life in Perspective

Setting Judges 4 and 5 alongside one another, the narrator encourages us to have a chapter-5 perspective on our own lives, as well as a chapter-4 one. The world lives by chapter 4, by sight; chapter 5 encourages us to live by faith, too. We may not know what God is doing in each event and part of our lives, but we can live with a continual note of "praise" for his victories, knowing that he is at work.

This keeps us from over-honoring ourselves in our successes, or despairing in our struggles. The story we tell of our lives should not be so much about us, as about him.

Apply

Why is it liberating to be able to look at our lives with a Judges-5 perspective?

What happens if we forget to?

Pray

Ask God to enable you to live by faith, rather than merely by sight. Ask him to help you do this in your struggles as well as your successes.

~ Notes and Prayers ~

Day
31

A Prophet and an Angel

Judges 6 v 1-24

The story is familiar now. Israel sins; God sends oppression; they cry out; God rescues them. Not this time...

A Surprising Response

Read Judges 6 v 1-10

How is the oppression worse than ever (v 2-6)?

When the Israelites cry out (v 7), what does God do (v 8)? Why is this surprising?

What does this messenger tell the people:

- *about what God has done?*
- *about how Israel should have responded?*
- *about what Israel has done?*

Why does God send a sermon before he sends salvation? It seems it's to show Israel that regret is not the same as repentance. They were crying out because they were sorry about the consequences of their sin—the oppression. But they were not sorry for the sin itself—for how they had wrecked their relationship with God. They didn't want to change their loves or get rid of their idols. They just wanted to have peace to continue in idolatry.

Read 2 Corinthians 7 v 10. Where does worldly sorrow (i.e. regret) lead? Where does repentance lead?

⊙ Apply

Think about the last time you said sorry to God. Were you regretful, or repentant?

Are you repeatedly sinning somehow, asking God to clear up the mess, and then carrying on? Will you repent?

A Timid Response

Read Judges 6 v 11-24

Don't miss God's grace here. There is no sign that the people responded to the sermon... but still God sends his angel to raise up his judge. He saves them before they turn back to him! God does not save us because we repent; we repent because he's begun to work in us and for us.

How does Gideon describe himself (v 15)?

How does the angel describe him (v 12, 14, 16)?

Both are right! In his own strength, Gideon will never be able to save Israel. In God's strength, he can do anything the LORD purposes.

Who is the angel of the LORD? Sometimes the angel speaks (e.g. v 12, 20); other times we are told the LORD is speaking (e.g. v 14, 16, 18). Gideon reacts as though he has seen someone very human (v 13), and then as though he has seen God himself (v 22). What is going on?!

This figure is both *not* the LORD, and yet also *is* the LORD! He looks like a man; yet has the power of God. And so there is good reason to see this person as God the Son. His concern even then was to bring salvation and peace to his people.

⊙ Apply

In what areas of your life do you need to remember to rely on the Lord today?

~ Notes and Prayers ~

Day
32

Among, Around, Within

Judges 6 v 25-40

God has called Gideon to be his next judge, despite Gideon's lack of courage. And to save the people, Gideon needs to defeat enemies at three levels.

The First Enemy

Read Judges 6 v 25-32

What does God tell Gideon to destroy and to build (v 25-26)?

Why is the identity of the owner of the altar a surprise?

Gideon's father has clearly taught his son about what God had done for Israel (v 13). But he has also been worshiping Baal and Asherah. The people have not abandoned worship of God for idols. Rather, they have combined worship of God with idols. This is the enemy among the people.

This brings Judges 6 close to home. We can happily sit in church, read our Bibles, talk about Jesus... and be controlled by idols. How do we know? Because if someone threatens our idols, we are furious (v 30). But remember God's sermon in verses 8-10. He wants not to remove our problems from our lives, so much as to remove our idols from our hearts.

It is worth asking ourselves, *What is there in my life which, if it were taken away from me, would make me feel like I couldn't carry on? What would I lash out about in order to keep?* This is a good way to begin to identify our idols.

⊙ Apply

What are your idols?

Will you tear them down and give that area of your life to God, finding your blessing and security in him?

The Second Enemy

Read Judges 6 v 33-35

What is the enemy around Israel (v 33)?

How does God strengthen Gideon, and with what result (v 34)?

The Third Enemy

Read Judges 6 v 36-40

What is Gideon still unsure of (v 36)?

This is the enemy within Gideon: doubt.

What is the fleece about?! It is not about guidance. Gideon lives in a world where forces of nature are worshiped as gods. He is asking for reassurance that the LORD is not merely a force of nature, but powerful over nature. He wants to understand God's nature, and so build up his faith.

Today, we live after God's self-revelation in his Son, recorded for us in the Bible (Hebrews 1 v 1-2). When we doubt God's promises, we don't "lay a fleece"; we can read Scripture, asking God to point us to his Son as we pray, "I do believe; help me overcome my unbelief!" (Mark 9 v 24).

⊙ Apply

How does this encourage/challenge how you deal with doubts/decisions?

~ Notes and Prayers ~

Day
33

Strength in Weakness

Judges 7 v 1-23

Here, we see God making his own servant weaker and weaker. Why would God—then and today—weaken his people, rather than his enemies?

Less is More

Read Judges 7 v 1-8a

Midian has terrorized Israel for seven years. And now Gideon's army is camped near them, ready for battle. Israel will need every man she can muster to defeat such a formidable enemy...

But what does God tell Gideon to do:

- *verse 3?*

- *verses 4-8?*

This is not advice included in any military manual!

Why does God want to reduce the army from 32,000 to 300 (v 2)?

We boast about the person or people who we think deserve glory and honor.

So why would thinking "her own strength has saved her" be Israel boasting "against" God?

As soon as we believe that we deserve credit for salvation—from Midian then, or from sin and death and hell eternally—we set ourselves up as alternative saviors, alternative deservers of praise. If Israel wins with an army of 32,000, they would be able to believe the army saved them. The lesson God will teach through the 300 is that victory is his.

How do Gideon's actions in verse 8 show great faith in God's strength?

Read 2 Corinthians 12 v 7-10

What has God done to Paul? Why?

Paul is saying, *Look how weak I am. It is clear that all that has been achieved has been achieved by God. How strong he is to be able to work through a weak man like me! Praise him!*

Victory Announced

Read Judges 7 v 8b-15

How does God reassure Gideon here?

Verse 15 shows us what happens when we allow God to reassure us of his strength and promises. We praise and worship God, and we act in radical obedience to him.

Victory Delivered

Read Judges 7 v 16-23

How many enemy soldiers do Gideon and his 300 kill?

This triumph is truly God-given, won despite and through Israel's weakness!

Pray

Father,

Help me not to want to be strong, or to win glory for myself.

Help me to embrace weakness, so that you can show your strength through me, and so I will remember to praise you.

Show me how I can obey you in my weakness so that you might show your greatness.

Amen.

~ Notes and Prayers ~

Day
34

The Dangers of Success

Judges 7 v 24 – 8 v 21

Previously, each judge's cycle has finished with a period of peace, followed by their death. But with Gideon, it's not as straightforward as that, because, as we'll see, he has failed to learn the "lesson of the 300," which God wanted to teach him and the people.

Remember the lesson of the 300: it is God who gives victory; and so it is God who deserves all the honor, glory and praise.

The Tribe

Read Judges 7 v 24 – 8 v 3

Gideon calls out the tribe of Ephraim to help him finish off Midian (7 v 24-25).

But what has annoyed the Ephraimites (8 v 1)?

Their criticism is born of having missed out on the glory of victory. But that glory belongs only to God! The LORD's charge that Israel loves to "boast against me" is proved correct.

The Towns

Read Judges 8 v 4-21

When Gideon asks the Israelite towns of Succoth and Peniel to help his exhausted men, how do these two towns respond (v 6, 8)?

They know Gideon hasn't yet caught the Midianite kings (v 5)—and that, if Gideon fails to defeat Midian utterly, then the enemy will regroup, return, and destroy any towns who helped Gideon.

They have also failed to learn the lesson of the 300—that God wins.

The Judge

How does Gideon answer the towns (v 7, 9)?

When he has captured the Midianite kings, how does he treat the two towns (v 13-17)?

Why is Gideon so violent? Because he feels these towns lack respect for him. His anger at them shows that he has forgotten that it is God who should be glorified, not him. He talks about how he will return in triumph (v 9). He does not say to these untrusting towns, *Yes, I'm weak. But God is strong. Trust him, not me, and join us!* He says, *You dare to doubt me? I'll show you my power when I return—then you'll give me the respect I deserve.*

Apply

Gideon's hunger for honor and his anger at being denied it show that success has been the worst thing for him.

Our hearts, too, are desperate to believe that we deserve praise and glory.

Do you ever grow frustrated at not getting recognition you feel you deserve?

What is your heart doing at that point?

In what areas of your life are you successful? How is that spiritually dangerous to you?

Pray

The best way to remember not to seek glory for ourselves is to give it to God! *Read Ephesians 2 v 8-10* and use it to fuel your praise of the Lord.

~ Notes and Prayers ~

Day 35

A Problematic Peace

Judges 8 v 22-31

Success, we saw in the previous devotional, is a poisoned chalice. And so is peace.

Read Judges 8 v 22-31

Who Rules?

What does Israel want Gideon to be, and why (v 22)?

In what way have the people forgotten the lesson of the 300?

At this point in Israel's history, God had decided to appoint judges to lead the people under him. If Gideon had said "yes," Israel would have had a king appointed by people, with rule then being passed on as a family inheritance. Kings were rich, wielded great influence, and had large families as a power base. The people wanted to be ruled by a man, not God, as Gideon understood (v 23).

How can, and why do, Christians today sometimes let a Christian leader take God's place?

Who Really Rules?

Verse 23 is, sadly, the last time Gideon remembers who God is, and who he is. He has said there, *I will not rule over you, because God rules over you. He deserves the honor, the glory and the influence.*

How do Gideon's actions in verses 24-27 and 29-31 then completely undermine his words?

What effect does all this have on Israel (v 27)?

God said the ephod-breastplate (v 27) was to be worn by the high priest in the tabernacle, the tent where God dwelled among his people (Exodus 28 v 29-30). It had two stones, the Urim and Thummim, which were used to ask God for guidance and deliver his decisions. At this time, the tabernacle was in Shiloh (Judges 18 v 31).

Why would it have been attractive to Gideon to put an alternative ephod in the town where he lived?

Israel is now at "peace" (8 v 28). In what sense is it a flawed peace?

How could Gideon turn down the kingship because he knew God is King—and then act like a king?! Because he knew something intellectually which had not really gripped his heart. He was failing to live out what he knew to be true.

Times of success, and times of peace, are dangerous! When we are struggling and weak, we know we need God. When all is well, it is very easy to look to others, and rely on and seek honor for ourselves.

Pray

Thank God that he is Ruler and Rescuer.

Ask him to help you not look elsewhere for blessing, or seek honor for yourself.

Talk to the Lord about any parts of your life where there is a disconnect between what you know about how he wants you to live, and how you are living.

~ Notes and Prayers ~

Day
36

How God Judges *Now*

Judges 8 v 29 – 10 v 5

In Gideon's judgeship, we saw some significant departures from the usual Judges cycle. In the life of the next ruler, we find there's no cycle at all.

Read Judges 8 v 29 – 9 v 57

The Anti-Judge

Why do the citizens of Shechem choose Abimelech as leader (9 v 2-3)?

How does Abimelech gain power (v 4-5)?

He has learned all the wrong lessons from his father, Gideon. He wants power for his own honor, not to help others. He brings death, not peace. He makes no pretense that God is King; he is happy to be crowned in God's place.

The Downfall

Humanly speaking, what brings Abimelech down (v 26-55)?

What do verses 23-24 and 56-57 tell us was going on "behind the scenes"?

God is silent throughout. But he is not absent. Through what looked like the normal course of events, he was acting in judgment. As Paul puts it, "The wrath of God is being revealed from heaven against all the godlessness and wickedness of men who suppress the truth by their wickedness" (Romans 1 v 18).

This chapter points us to three truths about God's present judgment:

- *It comes unseen.* No one at the time could have seen the spirit God sent.
- *It comes after a wait.* It took three years between Jotham's warning and judgment beginning (v 22-23).
- *It comes through the outworking of human sin.* For both Shechem and Abimelech, it was their greatest sins that proved their downfall. God's judgment on people is to give them over to the consequences of their sins.

How is the reality and nature of God's present judgment both encouraging and humbling?

The Salvation

Read Judges 10 v 1-5

What are we told about who Tola saved Israel from?

We're not! Or rather, we already know! Every other judge has saved Israel from others; Tola had to save Israel from themselves, from the sin and its consequences that we saw in chapter 9. The end of Gideon's life, and the whole of Abimelech's, show us that ultimately, God's people's greatest problem is... ourselves. So what we most need saving from is not what is around us, but what is within us—our own sin.

Pray

Read Titus 3 v 3-5

Thank God for his grace in saving you from yourself, and renewing you in his image. Ask him to continue to help you live under his rule, honoring and enjoying him.

~ Notes and Prayers ~

Day 37

Really Sorry?

Judges 10 v 6 – 11 v 11

With the next episode, focused on Jephthah, Israel's history returns to the repeated cycle:

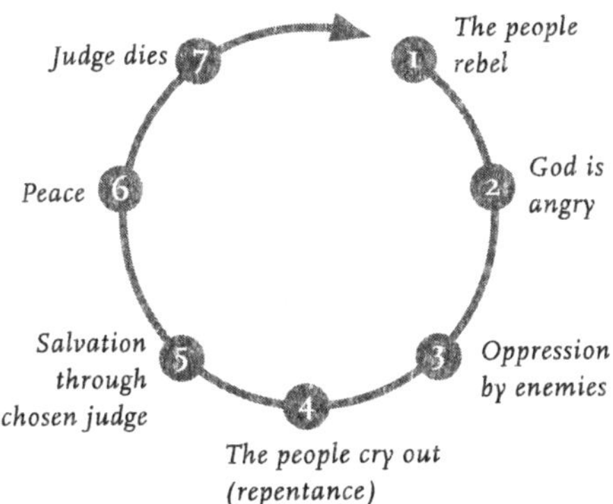

Read Judges 10 v 6-10

How do we see the first four stages of the Judges cycle here?

What would we expect to happen next?

The Twist

Read Judges 10 v 11-16

How does God answer (v 11-14)? What point is he making?

The Israelites understand the point. Their request in verse 15 is different from the one of verse 10. They say, *Do with us as you wish, though we still beg for mercy.* In verses 9-10, they simply wanted their distress removed. Now, they want relationship with God, whether or not their suffering ends. They want him, not just what he gives.

How does verse 16a show that Israel really has changed?

⊙ Apply

Repentance gets beneath the surface. The two signs of real repentance are:

• sorrow for sin, not just for its consequences

• sorrow over idolatrous motives, not just behavioral change

Reflect on some ways you have sinned over the last week. What idol were you worshiping at that point?

Have you actually repented of it?

Which aspects of God's perfection will you meditate on so that you love him more than you love what he gives?

The Gang Leader

Read Judges 10 v 17 – 11 v 11

In what ways is Jephthah an unlikely savior (11 v 1-3)?

Notice the people treat Jephthah just as they treated God. They rejected him (v 2), yet presume he will help them (v 5-6). They want him to rescue them, but not rule them as their head (v 6). Just as God did, Jephthah makes them ask more humbly, accepting that with rescue comes rule.

The judges all point to Jesus. So someone who rejects Jesus is rejecting God, however much they claim to know or respect him. And anyone who has been rescued by Jesus will have him as their ruler.

~ Notes and Prayers ~

Day
38

Pen Before Sword

Judges 11 v 12-29

Israel has turned back to God, and he has given them a judge, Jephthah. But Jephthah does not go to war with Israel's enemies immediately.

Read Judges 11 v 12-29

Jephthah is seeking a peaceful resolution—so he asks the king of Ammon, "What do you have against me that you have attacked my country?" (v 12). The king's answer, in verse 13, is that some of the land Israel now lives in formerly belonged to the Ammonites; and so Israel should "give it back peaceably."

Three Arguments

Verses 15-22 is a *historical* argument.

From whom, and how, did Israel gain the land now in dispute (v 19-22)?

The Ammonites (similarly named to, but completely different from, the Amorites!) had never lived in this land!

Next, Jephthah uses a *theological* argument (v 23-24).

What point is he making in v 23?

What should the Ammonites do (v 24)?

There are two ways of reading this. One is that Jephthah is *accommodating* himself to the Ammonites' pagan worldview—i.e. each nation's "god" gives that nation a portion of land—even though he knows this is wrong, because the LORD rules everything. The other is that Jephthah has *adopted* this view—that he knows so little of the LORD that he views him as one god among many.

Third, Jephthah deploys a *legal* argument (v 25-27). At the time Israel took this land in battle, no one challenged their right to it.

The Response

All three arguments prove that it is the Ammonites, not Israel, who are in the wrong.

How does the king of Ammon respond (v 28)?

How does God respond to the king of Ammon (v 29)?

Diplomacy is exhausted, so war is now inevitable. But Jephthah's use of the pen before the sword is important. Truth must be told, and peace sought, even though it does not always win the day. In this, Jephthah is pointing us to a greater leader...

Read 1 Peter 2 v 21-25

We follow a Savior whose truth was mocked, whose righteousness was ignored, yet who compromised on neither. Jephthah partially, and Christ supremely, give us an example of how to face unfair accusations.

⊙ Apply

The last time you dealt with an unfair accusation or criticism, how were you (or weren't you) like the Lord Jesus?

How will Jephthah's and Jesus' examples shape your response next time?

~ Notes and Prayers ~

Day
39

Vow, Death, War

Judges 11 v 29 – 12 v 8

God's Spirit has come upon Jephthah (v 29)—so the outcome of the coming battle is certain. But Jephthah doesn't understand this, with tragic consequences...

A Terrible Vow

Read Judges 11 v 29-33

What promise does Jephthah make (v 30-31)?

Why is it an unnecessary "deal" to offer?

The Lord gives total victory (v 32-33). Now, peace should follow. But...

A Terrible Death

Read Judges 11 v 34-40

This is a terrible story. Many have thought Jephthah had promised God an animal sacrifice. But the noun is not in the form appropriate for talking about animals. And if he had promised God the first animal out of his house, he would never have considered himself bound to sacrifice his daughter. Jephthah promised human sacrifice.

So why did Jephthah make, and keep, such a vow? God hates human sacrifice (Deuteronomy 12 v 31). But it seems Jephthah had been deeply de-sensitized to violence by the cruelty of the world around him. The world had squeezed him into its mold. Second, human sacrifice was how you could "buy off" a pagan god—Jephthah seems to have thought the LORD needed to be impressed and bought with a lavish "gift." The tragedy is that God had already been moved to save his sinful people (10 v 16), and had empowered Jephthah to bring this salvation (11 v 29).

⊙ Apply

Jephthah had listened to his culture far more, and his Scriptures far less, than he realized. And so he knew God far less well than he needed to. It is easy for us to see that in him; far harder for us to see it in ourselves. We need to ask ourselves two questions:

Am I regularly and humbly reading the Bible, asking God to show me my blind spots?

In what ways would I live more radically or restfully if I really believed God was completely committed to me, to love and bless me?

A Terrible War

Read Judges 12 v 1-8

Jephthah was diplomatic with those outside Israel (11 v 14-28); but here, he does not hesitate to strike out at those among God's people who oppose him. He treats God's people far worse than he treats the world.

⊙ Apply

How might you be too quick to judge fellow Christians?

Is there anyone in your church whom you are refusing to forgive, because deep down you like being able to look down on them or shun them?

How, and why, does this picture of real faith challenge you?

~ Notes and Prayers ~

Day 40

Samson's Birth

Judges 13 v 1-7

Samson, the last of the judges in this book, is famous for his long hair and his strength. But his story is much deeper and more intriguing than that.

Read Judges 13 v 1-7

What Sin is

What does Israel do once more (v 1)?

This phrase is repeated throughout Judges (e.g. 2 v 11; 10 v 6). It shows us that many of the things the Israelites did were not evil in their eyes—yet in God's, they were.

What does this teach us about what makes sin sin?

What does it teach us about the danger of sin?

At the heart of sin is idolatry—and idols are deceitful. They tell us, and they cause our society to tell us, that to worship them is sensible, careful and wise, when in fact we are doing evil in the only eyes in the universe that really matter.

⊙ Apply

Why is it liberating to know that God's eyes are the only ones which truly count?

How will your life today reflect the truth that God's eyes matter more than yours, and more than others'?

How God Works

What does the angel promise (v 3)?

Why is this impossible, humanly speaking (v 2)?

What does the angel tell her about how this child will live, and what he will do (v 4-5)?

The purpose of the Nazirite vow, laid out in Numbers 6 v 1-21, was to ask for God's special help during a crucial time; it was a sign that you were looking to God with great intensity and focus. Usually, the vow was made voluntarily and for a definite period of time.

How was this Nazirite vow different?

This is a special birth, because it is an impossible birth. So it points us to the most special of all births, over a millennium later. But Jesus' conception is not the only one that Samson's is similar to. God brought into the world through barren women Isaac, Samuel and John the Baptist (Genesis 11 v 30; 21 v 1-3; 1 Samuel 1 v 5-7, 19-20; Luke 1 v 7, 11-17). God has often worked through a child whose existence, humanly speaking, is impossible. In doing so, he shows that the outworking of his salvation is something that no human can manage; that he alone is the one who "gives life to the dead and calls things that are not as though they were" (Romans 4 v 17).

⊙ Apply

How does this reminder of who God is and how he works encourage and/or comfort you today?

~ Notes and Prayers ~

Day

41

Better than a Rulebook

Judges 13 v 6-25

How do you raise a baby who has been conceived through divine intervention, and who is destined to be God's means of rescuing his people?

Give us Rules

Read Judges 13 v 6-8

Why does Manoah want the angel to return (v 8)?

Some consider this to be a lack of faith—but notice that Manoah believes the promise will come true. His request is not for proof that the boy will be born, but for help with how to raise him.

Read Judges 13 v 9-18

When the angel returns, Manoah asks him for "the rule" for his son's life (v 12).

What extra information does he get (v 14)?!

In that culture, to eat with someone, or to know someone's name, was to establish relationship, with duties on both sides. It seems Manoah is still trying to get the angel to tell him more detailed rules about how to bring this boy up.

How does the angel respond to these attempts (v 16, 18)?

Whatever Manoah tries, the angel will not give him the rules he wants.

Better than Rules

Read Judges 13 v 19-25

Why would the angel have returned if he had nothing to say to Manoah? Manoah prayed for help, and the help was apparently refused. But in fact, Manoah did get the help he needed, but not in the form he was asking for. He wanted a "rule" (v 12)—he wanted regulations. He didn't get them...

What did the angel do instead (v 19-20)?

It's likely the angel of the LORD is actually the Son of God (see Study 31). So God is giving Manoah an unforgettable experience of his greatness and wonder. And, since they don't die in his presence (v 22-23), God is giving them an assurance of his goodness, too.

Manoah will not be given rules, because he is being given God. This is a message for all of us. We think we need rules, but we need to know God. God does not, and will not, give us a guidebook for every twist and turn, every doubt and decision. We don't get lots of prescriptions, and (unlike Manoah) we don't get an appearance from the angel of the LORD. We do, through the Holy Spirit, get God.

Apply

Are there ways in which you are not enjoying your relationship with the living God, because:

- *you are grudgingly obeying his "rules"?*
- *you are wishing he would give you some rules?*

Thank God now that you know *him.*

~ Notes and Prayers ~

Day
42

Wife and Strife

Judges 14 v 1-20

The story of Samson is a potent mix of sex, violence, death and power—exactly the stuff of a summer action film!

Finding a Wife

Read Judges 14 v 1-4

How is the woman Samson wants to marry described (v 1-2)?

Why don't his parents want him to marry her (v 3)?

Their issue is not with inter-racial marriage, but with inter-faith marriage. God had told his people that Israel were neither to ally with nor marry into peoples who did not know God (Exodus 34 v 15-16), because he knew that then his people would "prostitute themselves to their gods."

Yet here, the man who is supposed to be fighting the Philistines (Judges 13 v 5) is marrying into them. Samson is a leader who reflects Israel's real spiritual state. He is impulsive and unteachable, and has adopted the values and views of the Philistines.

Can you think of ways in the past when you, or your church, have taken on the surrounding culture's views about what is important in life?

Why is becoming like the culture so attractive for churches and believers?

Samson insists that "she's the right one for me" (literally, "she is right in my eyes," v 3b).

What do his parents, and Samson himself, not know (v 4)?

This verse is the key to understanding the whole story. God will use the weaknesses of Samson to bring about confrontation between the two nations. As the story goes on, we'll see everyone acting out of their own ungodly character—and God using it all to ensure that the deliverance of Israel from the Philistines begins.

Pray

Can you think of times when God has used your flaws to bring about good? Thank him for this grace.

Ask God to use you for his good purposes today, despite and even in your weaknesses.

Starting a Fight

Read Judges 14 v 5-20

As a Nazirite, Samson must not touch dead things, or drink alcohol. If he does, he must go straight to the tabernacle for cleansing.

How does he disdain his vow?

- *verses 5-9*
- *verse 10 ("feast" is literally "drinking party")*

How does Samson use his God-given gift of strength in verse 19?

Israel's judge fights not to deliver the people, but to settle his own debts.

Apply

What gifts have you been given by God? How could you use them today?

~ Notes and Prayers ~

Day 43

Violence and Treachery

Judges 15 v 1-20

We know enough about Samson by now to know that he is unlikely to respond peaceably to his fiancée marrying another man...

Vicious Cycle

Read Judges 15 v 1-8

How does the level of violence increase through these verses?

What picture do we get of:

- *the Philistines?*
- *Israel's judge?*

Again we see that Samson is just like God's enemies! His reactions and "solutions" are just the same as theirs.

Whose Side?

Read Judges 15 v 9-13

What is the Philistines' aim (v 10)?

Whose side does the tribe of Judah prove to be on? Why (v 11)?

They may bear the name of God's people, but Judah would rather live at peace with the world and worship their idols than be freed to worship God—and they would rather cut down their own rescuer than risk confrontation with the Philistines.

Apply

As God's people today, it is always easier to live like the world than to live under Jesus' rule. It is always more comfortable to ask Jesus to stop making demands on us than to accept the risk and cost of living for him.

Where are you under pressure to take the easier route in your life at the moment?

Whose Victory?

Read Judges 15 v 14-20

Why is Samson able to escape (v 14-15)?

Who does Samson give credit to for his victory (v 16)?

In verse 18, Samson (for the first time) speaks to the God who has chosen him, and empowered him. But his prayer is neither humble nor faithful; he basically demands that God helps him, and complains that God isn't doing so—which is remarkably clueless, given that God's Spirit has already rescued him from a lion, a lost bet, and a thousand Philistines.

Samson uses God's strength, but he doesn't depend on God except in extreme situations. He is a deeply flawed leader of a deeply flawed people... and yet, amazingly, God is working all the time to "begin the deliverance of Israel from the hands of the Philistines" (13 v 5).

Pray

Thank God for working for his people even when his people are working against him.

Pray that you would have eyes to see, and a heart to praise God, when he helps you. Ask him to help you prayerfully to depend on him today, whether it goes well or badly.

~ Notes and Prayers ~

Day 44

Defeated by "I"

Judges 15 v 20 – 16 v 21

"Samson led Israel for twenty years" (15 v 20). But it was not much of a rule, because—unlike the previous judges—he hadn't rescued Israel from its enemies.

Typical

Read Judges 15 v 20 – 16 v 3

This section sums Samson up. Because of his weakness for women (v 1), he's enticed into an extremely dangerous situation (v 2), and uses his God-given strength to escape (v 3). The more God blessed Samson with strength to fight his foes, the more Samson grew confident in his own invulnerability, and the more he lived as he saw fit. Samson's heart used God's blessings as a reason to forget God, not to obey him.

Apply

Success is spiritually dangerous!

How might this be a danger for you?

When do you most need to think, "This success in my life has come because of God's kindness to me, not because I am self-sufficient"?

Downfall

Read Judges 16 v 4-21

What causes Samson's downfall?

Why does Delilah betray him (v 5)?

Why did Samson stay with Delilah after verses 8-9?! Perhaps it gave him a high to be in danger; but more likely, he felt he so needed what Delilah gave him that he was in denial about her motives.

This couple are an extreme case of using one another rather than serving one another. They say to each other, "I am with you because I love you," but they mean, "I am with you because you are so useful to me." Doubtless there was a lot of passion; but it was all done out of a motive of self-enhancement, not self-giving. Samson was using Delilah to get sexual love and (probably) the thrill of danger; she was using him to get fortune and fame.

How does Samson end up (v 21)?

Why (v 20)?

It was never about the hair. It was about God and his generosity—which has now been withdrawn. Without God, Samson is nothing.

Apply

C.S. Lewis distinguished between two types of "love": "Need-love cries from our poverty; Gift-love longs to serve ... Need-love says of a woman [or man] 'I cannot live without her'; Gift-love longs to give her happiness."

Unless you have an experience of God's love that fulfills your deepest needs, you will tend to use other people to bolster or prove yourself.

How does this truth, seen so destructively in Samson and Delilah, challenge you in your relationships? How does it encourage you as a Christian?

~ Notes and Prayers ~

Day

45

Death and Victory

Judges 16 v 22-31

The man who had burned the Philistines' grain (15 v 4-5) is now reduced to grinding it (16 v 21). For the first time in Judges, God's chosen judge has been defeated.

Not about the Hair

Read Judges 16 v 22

Why did the Philistines let Samson's hair grow back? It must have been because they thought that God would never bless Samson again, given his broken vow. But God is not bound or limited by his people's obedience—he is faithful to his promises even when his people are unfaithful.

A Faithful Prayer

Read Judges 16 v 23-31

The true contest is Yahweh ("the LORD") versus Dagon, the god of the Philistines. Who is stronger? Who should Israel serve?

What appears to be the answer to those questions in verses 23-25?

How do verses 26-30 give the true answer?

At last, in verse 28, Samson shows true faith in God. There is a new-found humility. He recognizes Yahweh is sovereign. He acknowledges he depends on God for his strength. And he is prepared to die (v 30) to perform his God-given role, rather than use his God-given strength to save himself.

Apply

We do what we do only because of God's grace, and that grace is given so that we might do what is pleasing to him.

When, and why, do you find it easiest to forget this?

How will you make sure you remember?!

A Shadow of Jesus

The death of God's judge, to deliver his people, points us to the death of God's Son.

Both Samson and Jesus:

- were betrayed by someone close to them
- were handed over to Gentile oppressors
- were tortured and chained
- were asked to perform
- died with arms outstretched
- appeared completely struck down by their enemies (Dagon, and Satan), yet in their death crushed their enemy, breaking their power over God's people.

There are, though, two crucial differences:

- Samson was in Dagon's temple as a result of his own repeated disobedience. Jesus was on the cross as a result of his perfect obedience and our repeated disobedience.
- Samson's death began deliverance (13 v 5); Jesus' death achieved deliverance "once for all," a final rescue (see 1 Peter 3 v 18; Hebrews 10 v 10).

Pray

Spend time thinking about Jesus' death, in its similarities and differences to Samson's, and praise God for this greatest rescue.

~ Notes and Prayers ~

Day 46

Homemade Religion

Judges 17 v 1-12

In some ways, the end of Samson is the end of the Judges story. But there are four more chapters at the end of the book!

These last chapters are a departure from the earlier narrative structure. They give us two detailed episodes of what life was like in Israel during the times Israel rejected God. It is a bleak picture.

Making it Up

Read Judges 17 v 1-2

What is Micah like?

What is his mother like?

At least Micah's mother states that it is the LORD who gives blessings. This is a family that worships the God of Israel, in name...

Read Judges 17 v 3-12

What does Micah's mother decide to do with the now-returned silver (v 3)?

How much of the silver does she actually use for this purpose (v 4)?

What does Micah do next (v 5, v 7-12)?

God had told his people not to worship images (Exodus 20 v 4); he had told his people to be wholehearted in their devotion to him, as he was wholehearted in his commitment to them (Exodus 19 v 3-6); he had told them they should meet with him and make sacrifices to him in his tabernacle, which at this point was in Shiloh (Judges 18 v 31); he had told them that only those of the tribe of Levi were to be priests, based in particular towns.

How is the end of verse 6 therefore a good summary of Micah's religion?

The Image Problem

The real issue in worship-by-images is the desire to shape and revise God—to refuse to let God "be himself" in our lives. So we worship a distorted image of God whenever we say, "I like to think of God as..." or, "I can't believe in a God who..." or, more subtly, when we simply don't think about the implications of God's revelation in our own lives.

Why is this such a problem? Because it makes it impossible to have a truly personal relationship with God. In relationship with a real person, they can contradict you and upset you and make demands on you, and you have to wrestle with that and deal with that. When we "re-image-ine" God, we are swapping the real God for a much more comfortable, but non-existent, one.

⊙ Apply

How might you be tempted to fall into the mistakes of Micah and his mother:

- *in revising who God is?*
- *in holding some of your life back from serving him?*
- *in ignoring the way he has told you to worship him?*

~ Notes and Prayers ~

Day

47

How Not to Live

Judges 17 v 13 – 18 v 31

Micah has now completed his homemade religious set-up: a shrine, an image, and a Levite priest.

Read Judges 17 v 13

What is the goal of his religious activity?

Enter Dan

Read Judges 18 v 1-26

Why is the tribe of Dan homeless (v 1)?

They are in this situation because they had failed to trust God and take their land, and so had been "confined to the hill country" (1 v 34). They didn't listen to what God really said, so they now ask a pagan Levite working at an idolatrous shrine for guidance, decide God has blessed them (18 v 10), and set out to take the land (v 11-12). Dan's approach to God is very similar to Micah's.

Empty-Handed

What do the Danites take from Micah's house (v 14-21)?

How does Micah respond (v 22-24)?

Everything Micah had could be taken away from him—and he had nothing else. All that he trusted in had gone, and he could not get them back (v 25-26).

In the end, self-made religion will disappoint. Whatever we make into our god will not deliver. The person who makes career their god will eventually find their route to blessing blocked by someone who is "too strong"; the person who makes image their god will find that time is an enemy who is "too strong." Ultimately, death removes all the false gods we look to for blessing.

Everyone is a worshiper. And there is only one who will never be taken away from us—the One of whom we can say, with Peter, "To whom shall we go? You have the words of eternal life" (John 6 v 68). When we worship Jesus, we find blessing—but we only truly experience his blessing when we say to him, "Jesus, without you, what else do I have? You are my everything."

Apply

Why is it wonderfully liberating to realize that Jesus is all we need?

How will you enjoy him today?

What are the things which you find easy to worship instead of him?

Exit Dan

Read Judges 18 v 27-31

This is a depressing end to the story. Here's a tribe born into God's people Israel, but who now live outside God's land, do not listen to his word, and worship him in a way entirely at odds with what he has commanded.

Pray

Heavenly Father,

Please save me from Dan's mistakes; enable me to trust you, listen to you, and worship you today.

Amen.

~ Notes and Prayers ~

Day 48

A Levite and his Lover

Judges 19 v 1 – 20 v 7

This second ground-level story at the end of Judges is very dark and unremittingly tragic. Israel remembered it as a deeply shameful episode (read Hosea 9 v 9; 10 v 9).

Read Judges 19 v 1-30

The Shame of Gibeah

The opening verse introduces us to another Levite, who has a concubine—a second-class wife, kept as a sex-servant.

What does the concubine do (v 2)?

What do you make of her father's decision to allow the Levite to have her back (v 3-10)?

What do you make of the old Ephraimite man's conduct?

- *verses 16-21*
- *verses 22-24*

What happens to the concubine in Gibeah (v 25-28)?

The Levite seems totally unconcerned—he sends her out (v 25), and then goes to bed until the morning (v 27), and then speaks to her as if to an animal (v 28). Why then does he send her body parts round Israel (v 29)? Because he wants vengeance, not for the treatment of the woman, but for the loss of what he sees as his property. The narrator is quite clear that no one in this episode is free of guilt. No one has not sinned.

Read Genesis 19 v 1-11

What are the similarities between Sodom and Gibeah?

Sodom is the great Old Testament example of rebellion against God that rightly brings upon itself the judgment of God.

So what do the events in Gibeah show us about God's people?

Changing the Details

Read Judges 20 v 1-7

How does the Levite edit his account of what happened to make himself sound innocent?

It is worth remembering that these things really happened, among God's people. These are our spiritual ancestors. They show us, to an extent, ourselves. We may have secrets buried deep that bear resemblance in some (perhaps small) way to the Gibeonites' conduct. Or we may, like the Levite, have failed to prevent them. All of us will have told ourselves and others a better story about ourselves than the whole truth will reveal. All of us have at times lived as though there is "no king" (19 v 1).

Pray

Are there:

- *well-buried secrets you need to confess, mourn, and repent of?*
- *ways you've told yourself a story which is better than the truth—ways you need to be honest, and confess?*

Despite who we are, God is full of grace to us. Thank him that, whatever lies in your past or in your future, his mercy is sufficient to cover it. *Read Psalm 103.*

~ Notes and Prayers ~

Day

49

Civil War

Judges 20 v 8-48

As they gather to decide what to do about Gibeah, Israel is united as at no time since Judges 3. They are "as one" (v 8). All apart from the tribe of Benjamin, that is.

War Comes

Read Judges 20 v 8-16

What do the people commit to doing (v 8-11)?

What do they do before going to battle against Benjamin (v 12-13)?

How do the Benjamites respond (v 13b-16)?

Why do they not just turn over the guilty men to face justice? Most likely because of the idol of kindred: the attitude of, "My family/country, right or wrong." When we put our blood or racial ties or community above the common good and the moral order, we make a god of "our own people."

Apply

Can you think of ways you have done, or are doing, this when it comes to your family or community?

War Won

Read Judges 20 v 17-48

After several battles, what happens to the Benjamite army in the end (v 41-47)?

The victory is won... but what happens next (v 48)?

This is not justice; this is genocide. It is the work of bitterness, which demands not one eye but two, in revenge for every eye lost. Bitterness always flowers into vindictiveness, on a national level, but also on a personal one. At that level, the destructiveness is still real, though scaled down.

How to Forgive

The only way to avoid bitterness and angry resentment is to practice forgiveness. How can we do this? Three ways:

1. *Realize what forgiveness is.* Forgiveness is granted before it is felt (Luke 17 v 3-6). It is a promise to not bring up the wrong with the person, or with others, or in your own thoughts; not to dwell on the hurt or nurse ill-will.
2. *Realize how forgiveness is possible.* We will only forgive if and as we see and feel the reality of God's massive and costly forgiveness of us through Christ. Only knowing how vast our debt to God was, and that it is now canceled, will enable us to have perspective on someone else's debt to us (Matthew 18 v 21-35).
3. *Forgive before we try to be reconciled* (Mark 11 v 25). That way we won't approach someone angrily, or try to "beat" them. We will be able truly to seek to restore the relationship.

⊙ Apply

How is knowing Christ's forgiveness of you shaping your treatment of others?

Is there anyone you need to forgive, as God has forgiven you?

~ Notes and Prayers ~

Day

50

Wives for Benjamin

Judges 21 v 1-24

The war is over. All that remains of the tribe of Benjamin is six hundred men, hiding in the desert (20 v 47).

The Problem

Read Judges 21 v 1-7

What have the men of Israel sworn (v 1)?

Given that they have also killed all the Benjamite women, what is the consequence of this (v 3, 6-7)?

Who do they seem to blame in verse 3?

What other oath have the men of Israel taken (v 5)?

"Why has this happened?" they ask (v 3). They should know! It was their rash oath, and their massacre of their Benjamite brothers and sisters, which has caused this. But instead of pointing the finger at themselves, they suggest it is somehow God's fault.

Apply

It is easier to put God in the wrong than to engage in self-reflection. But if we do this, we will never confess our sins, or learn from our mistakes.

Look over your last week. Is there anything that, on reflection, you need to confess?

The Solutions?

Read Judges 21 v 8-24

The men of Jabesh Gilead had not attended the assembly (v 8-9)—and, given Israel's second oath (v 5), this seems to present them with a solution to the problem of Benjamin's future.

What do Israel do (v 10-14)?

What is the problem (v 14)?

What is the next "solution" (v 2, 19-22)?

How does this get round the oath (v 23)?

An assembly which had gathered to do justice for a single raped and murdered woman ends up planning and promoting the murder of a whole town, and the abduction and rape of the girls of two towns.

Solutions and Problems

Every time they try to "purge the evil" (20 v 13) from their society, the Israelites make the problem worse. This is the problem with human solutions to what is essentially a spiritual problem—evil. There is no military campaign or state policy that can solve a problem which resides in the human heart. Only a revival of faith can do this. But Israel do not recognize that they are as much under oppression and slavery as if they had a foreign master. They are spiritually in darkness, but they don't realize it.

Pray

Ask God to give revival to your church.

Tell God about some issues or decisions you are facing.

Ask God to help you trust in and obey him, rather than doing what seems sensible or logical in your own eyes.

~ Notes and Prayers ~

Day 51

In Search of the King

Judges 21 v 25

And so we reach the end of the book of Judges. It has not been an easy read. But the narrator leaves us with a summary comment which is also a ray of hope.

Read Judges 17 v 6; 18 v 1; 19 v 1; 21 v 25

What does the narrator say is the problem with Israel?

What does he suggest is the solution?

Israel had no King

Think back over the whole of Judges.

How have we seen that the people are the problem?

What have we seen about the kind of solution God would need to provide?

If nothing else, Judges shows us that though we are the problem, we cannot be our own solution. We need to search for a king, just as Israel did. But by the end of the book, we have come to wonder whether and how a mere human king can be enough. The subsequent Old Testament history confirms that even the best kings, such as David, are not enough.

Judges is humbling, because it shows us we need a deliverer who:

- comes without being called for, since humans are not really seeking God.
- chooses his people, because we would never choose him.
- achieves our rescue entirely himself, since we are incapable of contributing to it.
- can "purge" us of the evil (20 v 13) in our hearts, not just in our societal structures.
- does not die, leaving us to our own flaws and failings once more.

We need a king, but a greater king with a greater deliverance than any human can be or perform.

The King we Need

Read Psalm 96 v 11-13

Here, the word "judge" is used in its original sense of "rule with justice"—as the leaders of Judges should have, but (in the main) failed to. The psalmist sees that it will require God himself to come and be our judge.

All of us search for a king—someone or something to rule us, someone or something to rescue us and bless us. There is only one man who provides what we are looking for—who came uninvited, called his people, died alone to rescue us, changes our hearts by his Spirit, and who rules beyond death for ever. Judges leaves us aching for a king; it leaves us appreciating the King, our Lord Jesus.

Pray

Thank God for two or three encouragements and challenges for your own life that you are taking from the book of Judges.

Then spend time simply thanking God for King Jesus.

~ Notes and Prayers ~

Day
52

Grace and Peace

Ephesians 1 v 1-2

Ephesians is packed with stunning passages. Every chapter yields fresh treasures. Digging them up will enrich your life, and increase your confidence in sharing them.

Read Ephesians 1 v 1-2

From and To

Who is the letter from, and to (v 1)?

Paul begins all his letters by reminding us that he is "an apostle of Christ Jesus." And this matters greatly—he is writing as one of Christ's authorized and empowered witnesses to proclaim the eternal and cosmic will of God. We cannot ignore or dismiss any of what he says!

The earliest manuscripts don't include the name "Ephesus." Since the letter's style is general (it doesn't have any reference to local people or issues), it's likely it was a circular letter to all the churches in the region (now western Turkey). These churches would have been planted from Ephesus, where Paul had been senior pastor for 2 ½ years. Ephesus was a cosmopolitan and commercial city, devoted to the temple of the Greek goddess Artemis.

Read Acts 19 v 1 – 20 v 1

What did the new Christians in Ephesus do that showed their commitment to following Christ as their Lord?

What caused Paul to end his time there?

What and Where

What does Paul wish his readers (v 2)?

What, does he say, is the source of these two things (v 2)?

The first was customarily a Gentile greeting—the second, a standard Jewish greeting. Paul combines them here (his God-given gospel was, of course, for both Jew and Gentile); and in doing so, he introduces some massively important themes in this letter. He will celebrate God's "grace" as his undeserved kindness and the origin of all our blessings in Christ—*read v 6; 2 v 7.*

And "peace" is the summary of all the blessings resulting from being reconciled to God and to each other in Christ—*read 2 v 14-17.* If grace is the *origin* of God's plan to gather us into the blessings of his church in Christ, then peace is the *result* of it, demonstrating in the spiritual realms the triumphant wisdom of the gospel of Christ crucified—*read 3 v 10-12.*

Apply

How does verse 2 excite you about:

- *your life as a Christian?*
- *reading this letter?*

Pray

Thank God that, in his grace, he sent his Son, the Lord Jesus, to bring us peace. Pray that as you study Ephesians, you would appreciate more fully all that it means for you to be "in Christ."

~ Notes and Prayers ~

Day
53

Every Blessing

Ephesians 1 v 3

In the original Greek, verses 3-14 of Ephesians chapter 1 are one long, breathless sentence. It's an avalanche of praise for God. And Paul begins by summarizing what he's so excited about.

Read Ephesians 1 v 3

Where?

Where has God "blessed us" (v 3)?

This is a crucial phrase that Paul repeats five times in Ephesians—we need to grasp it in order to understand the letter.

The heavenly realms are the spiritual dimension in which God and all spiritual powers are dwelling. They are not just heaven, they are not just earth, and they are not only a future reality. The heavenly realms are the spiritual dimension where Christ reigns (1 v 20) and where we have already been raised to be seated with him (2 v 6). The "spiritual blessings" we enjoy are the eternal treasures of personal reconciliation with God—and we enjoy them from the time we first trust in Christ.

What?

Why is "every" a stunning word here?

How do we access these blessings, according to this verse?

Scan-read Ephesians 1 v 3-14

How many times do you spot "in Christ" (or "in him" or "through him")?

God wants us to remember that we owe everything to his Son. We're blessed not just "through" Christ, as the mechanism for receiving blessing, but personally "in" Christ—our blessings are to be enjoyed with him, in relationship with him.

When?

When do we enjoy all these? We shall only enjoy them fully in glory in the future—but we experience them in part now, and they should fill our hearts with joy even now. All we have to do to experience the blessings fully is... die. Even I can manage that!

Apply

How does this verse change your view of yourself, and of your death?

Christians have different gifts and ministries, but all are equally blessed in Christ.

Why do we find it easy to forget this (of ourselves and of others)?

How does remembering this give us a more settled and satisfied sense of our own identity?

God has given each Christian everything to enjoy in eternity.

How does that excite and comfort you today?

Pray

Remember that the truths of verse 3 cause Paul to urge us to "praise ... the God and Father of our Lord Jesus Christ." Do so now!

~ Notes and Prayers ~

Day
54

Chosen for Adoption

Ephesians 1 v 4-6

The nineteenth-century English preacher Charles H. Spurgeon said, "Election sets the heart on fire with enthusiastic delight in God." That may surprise you! But Paul agrees. Let's see why...

Read Ephesians 1 v 4-6

Chosen

What did God do "in him" (v 4)? When did he do it?

What did God do (v 5)? Why (end v 5)?

Long before we ever chose to follow Jesus, God the Father "chose us." This is what Paul calls predestination (v 5) or (elsewhere) election. And it is what Jesus taught, too—*read John 6 v 37; Matthew 11 v 28.*

God's election of sinners for salvation is part of his sovereignty over everything (Ephesians 1 v 11). And whenever we pray, we are acknowledging that God is in control; whenever we pray for someone to be saved, we're (at least unconsciously) recognizing that God is in control of saving people.

But God choosing people can seem to undermine evangelism (God will save those he has chosen anyway), undermine our humility (we're the chosen ones), and undermine our holiness (we're saved anyway).

Paul helps us with each objection. First, God uses our evangelism to save his elect (read Acts 18 v 9-10). Since he has chosen many, our evangelism is the joyful privilege of finding his elect with his gospel, like miners digging for gold in a pit.

Second, election keeps us humble because we were chosen "before the creation of the world"—we're not saved because we turned out to be cleverer or more deserving. Since he first chose us, we can only ever be humble.

Third, we were chosen "to be holy and blameless in his sight" (v 4). Saved through Jesus, we'll want to be like Jesus—holy.

Apply

How have these verses changed your view of election and predestination?

Do you need to use the doctrine of election to encourage your heart to:

- *desire to evangelize more?*
- *grow in humility?*
- *advance in holiness?*

Adopted

What did God choose us for (v 4)?

In Old Testament Israel, the firstborn son inherited the land. Adopted "to sonship," God has chosen to give us all of his Son's privileges. In Christ, we are brought right into the family of the triune God, able to whisper into the ear of our Father!

Pray

The great theologian J.I. Packer writes, "You sum up the whole of New Testament religion if you describe it as the knowledge of God as one's holy Father."

Spend time speaking to your Father now, thanking him for what he has given you in Christ, and asking him for the help you need to live as his child today.

~ Notes and Prayers ~

Day
55

Redeemed by His Blood

Ephesians 1 v 7-10

In the Bible, "redemption" means liberation from slavery upon the payment of a ransom. And in Christ "we have redemption through his blood" (v 7).

The biblical background to the idea of redemption is in Exodus, when the Israelites were slaves in Egypt. They were liberated from captivity under Pharaoh, and from God's judgment upon their sin, by the blood of sacrificed "Passover" lambs that were killed in the place of the Israelite firstborn sons.

Redeemed From...

Read Ephesians 1 v 7-10; 2 v 1-3

What have we been redeemed from (2 v 1-3)?

You were unable to break free from sin. You were imprisoned by it. But now you are free. And though we often wander back into the filthiness of our cells, "in him" the door of the cell has been permanently opened by Jesus, who patiently keeps walking us out into the light again.

What is this redemption "through" (1 v 7)?

What does it result in (middle of v 7)?

For God to allow such a sacrifice to pay for our sins is grace. For God to *provide* such a sacrifice is amazing grace! For God to *become* such a sacrifice is grace beyond our comprehension! He truly has "lavished on us" the "riches of [his] grace" (v 7-8).

We are freed from fear—Satan cannot successfully demand we be punished for our sins. And we are freed from guilt—we are not a wretched disappointment to God, and we do not have to try to impress him (or anyone), because our sins are now pardoned and the record of our sins is permanently deleted.

Redeemed For...

God has "made known to us the mystery"—the secret—"of his will." God grants us the extraordinary privilege of knowing his eternal plans—what it is that will happen "when the times reach their fulfillment" (v 10)!

And where is everything heading (end v 10)?

The divine Architect has published his glorious construction plan. He has laid the foundation in the death and resurrection of Christ. And the completion of his glorious new creation is now just a matter of time. Notice the focus of his plan is not us, but Christ. And no part of his plan is uncertain or risky. We don't need to worry about the things we don't know and can't control.

⊙ Apply

Are you living in fear or under guilt because of your sin? How does verse 7 both liberate and challenge you? How will you see yourself differently?

Are you living in anxiety because you're afraid of the future? How does verse 10 both liberate and challenge you? How will you live differently?

~ Notes and Prayers ~

Day 56

Sealed for Inheritance

Ephesians 1 v 11-14

We have been chosen for adoption by the Father. We have been redeemed for unity by the Son. Today, we find that we have been sealed for inheritance by the Spirit.

Read Ephesians 1 v 11-14

The Spirit's Work

How do people become "included in Christ" (v 13)?

What happened to every Christian "when [they first] believed" (v 13)?

What does this guarantee (v 14)?

A "seal" was the mark of ownership and protection which in Roman culture was often branded upon cattle. Paul is saying that it is as though every Christian has been marked by God's Spirit with a spiritual UV marker pen, marking them out as those belonging to God.

Moreover, the Spirit is the first installment—the deposit—that guarantees the full "payment" of life spent enjoying God in heaven, because he is God within us. He is like the delicious first course of the sumptuous spiritual feast to come, in the new creation.

Remembering this will enable us to avoid two common errors. First, we'll avoid thinking that our joy in the presence of God is only for the future—we can already enjoy something of heaven now, through the Spirit who dwells within us. Second, we'll avoid thinking that our current experience is all there is—in fact, the best is yet to come!

Don't miss how secure your future is, if you believe the gospel. The election of the Father, the redemption of the Son and the indwelling of the Spirit are all irreversible.

Apply

How do the words "sealed" and "deposit" help you to appreciate the work of God's Spirit in you?

The Christian's Response

Two magnificent phrases that each appear four times in v 1-14 tell us how to respond to all that we have seen.

First, all this is happening according to his will (v 1, 5, 9, 11). We can rejoice that God is accomplishing his plan. We're not accidents, and our lives are not pointless.

And how should we react to knowing the plan and appreciating our blessings (v 14, see also v 3, 6, 12)?

We are not merely to grit our teeth and get through life. We're consciously to revel in God's gracious blessings. When we do that, we will live to the praise of his glory as we appreciate the exquisite joy of being saved.

Pray

I praise you, my God and the Father of my Lord Jesus Christ, for blessing me and my church family in the heavenly realms with every spiritual blessing in Christ.

Thank you for adopting me. Thank you for redeeming me. Thank you for sealing me. Thank you that I can live to the praise of your glory.

Amen.

~ Notes and Prayers ~

Day 57

Lessons in Prayer

Ephesians 1 v 15-16

Paul now reveals to the Ephesian church what he's been praying for them. As we explore Paul's prayer points, we'll be learning a lot about why, how, and what to pray.

Read Ephesians 1 v 15-16

Paul's Fuel

Paul begins, "For this reason...," meaning, *Because of what I've just said in verses 1-14 about God gathering his chosen, redeemed and sealed people together under Christ...*

And what has Paul "heard about" when it comes to his first readers (v 15)?

In other words, they bear the telltale cross-shaped birthmark of God's true children. They have the vertical dimension of faith in the Lord Jesus. And they have the horizontal dimension of love for all of God's people, rather than only for those who are like them, or those who could be beneficial to them.

Real Christians always demonstrate growth in both of these dimensions—faith in Christ and love for all believers.

How do you think the great truths of verses 3-14 cause us to continue to have faith in Christ, and grow in love for Christians?

Paul's Thanks

As Paul thinks about the truths of v 3-14, and considers the cross-shaped evidence of the living faith of the Ephesian church...

What does he do (v 16)?

The apostle is setting us an example for our own prayers. He prayed unceasingly—not just sporadically, but regularly; generously—not just for himself, but for others; and gratefully—appreciating God's work in their lives and church, and not just in his own. It poses a challenge for us: do we, and will we, pray like this for other people?

Read Matthew 6 v 9-13

What is significant about the fact that Jesus used the words "our," "us" and "we" rather than "my," "me" and "I"?

Jesus wants us to learn to care more about our Christian brothers and sisters than ourselves—just as Paul does in Ephesians 1.

⊙ Apply

To what extent do your prayers share the hallmarks of Paul's in verse 16. Are they:

- *regular?*
- *generous?*
- *grateful?*

⊙ Pray

Think of a few Christians in your church whose lives reveal their "faith in the Lord Jesus and ... love for all God's people."

Read verses 3-14. Praise God that each verse is true of each of those people. Use these verses to thank God for these brothers and sisters by name.

Could you make time to pray for these fellow Christians a few times each day this week?

~ Notes and Prayers ~

Day 58

What to Pray For

Ephesians 1 v 17-20

Next, we learn from what Paul prays for. He is asking the Father to give the Ephesians deeper knowledge of three things that they already have in Christ.

Read Ephesians 1 v 17-20

To Know Him

What does Paul "keep asking" the Father to do for the Ephesians believers (v 17)?

What will be the outcome of this (v 17)?

Paul knew that the greatest blessing that anyone can experience is to know God, and to know him better every day (see Philippians 3 v 8). As J.I. Packer puts it, "We are cruel to ourselves if we try to live in this world without knowing about the God whose world it is and who runs it." God is the source of the deepest satisfaction and joy to his adopted children.

To Know Hope

What needs to be "enlightened" (Ephesians 1 v 18)?

What will this enable us to "see" (v 18)?

Paul knows the way we "see" this world is informed by the affections of our hearts. He does not pray that God would alter the circumstances of the Ephesians' lives, but that he would alter the way they see the circumstances of their lives. He wants them to see everything with the eyes of faith, trusting that what God has promised, he will do.

When Christians "see" life in this way, they live a life of "hope" that is unique in this world, because they know they are heading to God's "glorious inheritance." And don't miss what his "inheritance" is. It is... us! God is waiting to welcome us into his home. We won't sneak in through the back door. We'll be welcomed at the front gate.

But... will it really happen? Will our disintegrated bodies really be reunited with our souls and live forever in the new creation? Paul knows that we need...

To Know Power

How strong is the power that is at work within "us who believe" (v 19-20)?

How does this give us confidence that we really will live with God forever?

We could say that God has practiced resurrecting us in raising Jesus. He's done it before, so we know he can do it again.

Pray

We need to learn to pray as Paul does—for ourselves and for other believers. Let's not just pray for them to know earthly peace and prosperity, health and happiness. Let's pray for them to experience the huge spiritual privileges of knowing God better, of knowing the hope to which he's called us, and of knowing the power which he has committed to bringing us home to be with him.

Call to mind the Christians you thanked God for at the end of the previous study. Pray for them now as Paul did for his friends in Ephesus.

~ Notes and Prayers ~

Day
59

Far Above All Others

Ephesians 1 v 18-23

Many Christians are dangerously oblivious to satanic powers. The Bible says Satan is real, furious and dangerous. But in recognizing this, we can end up becoming too afraid...

That seems to have been the Ephesians' problem. They were afraid that spiritual opposition was too strong; they knew their spiritual opponents were more powerful than them; and so they worried that they would not make it home to heaven.

Do you think you tend to underestimate or overestimate the power of the devil?

What effect does that have on your view of your Christian life and your future?

Read Ephesians 1 v 18-23

Dominion

God's power did not only work in Christ to raise him from the dead (v 20)...

What else did it do (v 20-21)?

When we consider Satan and evil spiritual powers, why is v 22 reassuring?

The point is simply this: no one can get remotely close to taking us away from our Savior. Indeed, incredible though it sounds, God has "appointed him to be head over everything *for the church*" (v 22, my italics). Christ rules everything. And he governs this world for the benefit of the church so that the church will become more like him, and will one day be with him.

How does the start of verse 23 explain why Christ cares so much about the church?

As Paul will point out later in the letter, "no one ever hated their own body, but they feed and care for their body, just as Christ does the church" (5 v 29). We will most certainly be raised to life with him, because he himself was raised to life and we are his living body. Our head cannot be separated from his body!

Presence

So what does every church enjoy (v 23)?

God is intensely present in every church. All God's resurrection power is being employed to gather churches together, and then keep churches trusting Christ until they physically arrive to join the great heavenly gathering around the throne of Christ. It is unimaginable power, and should give us unlimited confidence!

⊙ Apply

How have these verses given you:

- *a bigger view of Jesus?*
- *a greater view of your own church?*
- *a larger confidence in your future?*

⊙ Pray

Continue to pray as you did at the end of the previous study, enjoying the confidence that your Head is at the right hand of the One to whom you pray.

~ Notes and Prayers ~

Day
60

Our Natural Selves

Ephesians 2 v 1-3

In chapter 2, Paul explains how we are brought together under Christ. First, we're reconciled to God (v 1-10); second, we're reconciled to each other (v 11-22). But to understand how we were reconciled to God, we must begin by seeing why we needed to be reconciled to God.

What we're Really Like

We all tend towards an inflated view of ourselves. We are like grimy miners down in a pit, comparing ourselves with each other and imagining ourselves relatively clean.

Read Ephesians 2 v 1-3

How does the Bible describe us (v 1)?

Spiritually, we were born dead to God, because we were born as sinners. Spiritual life was impossible for us—corpses can't help themselves.

What three "tyrants" does Paul say hold us captive, so that we can't escape from our sin and our death (v 2-3a)?

It is not only teenagers who are driven by their peer culture—we all are. Our instinct is to follow "the ways of this world," whether that be a traditional, duty-based, self-righteous worldview that rejects the gospel, or the emergent, feelings-based, individually autonomous one that also rejects the gospel.

"The ruler of the kingdom of the air" is Satan. Unbelievers are not generally possessed by Satan or his demons—but every unbeliever is willingly persuaded by his lies because they are "disobedient" (v 2). Naturally, we want the lies of the devil to be true so that we can carry on sinning.

"Our flesh" does not mean just our physical body but our whole human nature. We are, by nature, held captive by our own cravings: our appetite for selfish luxury, or self-indulgent popularity, or proud self-glorification.

Paul is showing us that our sin was very natural to us. It held us captive—and we liked it that way. It's not only that we were unable to break free of this triple bondage, but also that we didn't want to.

What we Really Deserve

What were we all "deserving of" (end of v 3)?

All of us will spend eternity in God's presence. His people will be flooded with his undeserved blessing; his enemies will be filled with the torment of his deserved anger.

Remember, Paul has wonderful news to share of God's grace. But we will never truly rejoice in it until we recognize how appalling our natural condition really is without Christ.

⌄ Apply

Before you became a Christian, how were the three "tyrants" at work in you?

Have you ever really appreciated that, by nature, all that your abilities and achievements deserved was "wrath"? What difference does accepting this make to your view of:

- *yourself?*
- *your Savior?*

~ Notes and Prayers ~

Day
61

The God of Rich Mercy

Ephesians 2 v 4-10

Paul has shown us that we were "dead" in our sins (v 1). Now he jubilantly celebrates God's grace in reaching down to us in our utter helplessness.

Read Ephesians 2 v 1-7

But God...

Given verses 1-3, why is the "But" at the beginning of verse 4 such a wonderful word?

The first three verses of chapter 2 are all about what we have done, and what we therefore deserve. The next four verses are all about what God has done, and what we therefore enjoy.

So what has God done for us (v 4-7)?

Four key Bible words in this passage celebrate the beauty of God's character, revealed in sending his Son:

- *Love (v 4):* God's commitment to bless us for ever in Christ
- *Mercy (v 4):* God withholding the punishment we deserved because Christ endured it for us on the cross
- *Grace (v 5, 7, 8):* God generously giving us what we need in the obedience of Christ even unto death

- *Kindness (v 7):* God's compassion in shrinking himself down to become one of us to exchange places with us on the cross!

Paul does not dwell on the cross here, but on the resurrection. His focus is less on our guilt and need of justification, and more on our alienation from God and need of a resurrection that was accomplished on the cross and then secured in the resurrection.

With Christ

What three things has God done for us "with Christ" (v 5-6)?

In Christ, our representative King, we've already been raised... accepted into heaven... and seated at the Father's right hand (see 1 v 20-21). Since, in Christ, heaven is now our present dwelling, it must be our future destination. Our seats are reserved by Jesus and secured in Jesus.

Why did God do all this (2 v 7)?

This isn't just an exercise in tidying up the mess, or in putting down the rebellion. God's plan is for ever to pour out a torrent of kindness upon us. Every day of eternity we shall be flooded with fresh blessings of his grace to explore and enjoy, and to prompt us to praise our Savior.

How does the reality of verses 1-3 enable us to appreciate the wonder of verses 4-7?

Apply

How do these verses make you feel about yourself, and about God?

How will the reality that you are "seated with" Christ in heaven change the way you see your life today?

Pray

Re-read verses 4-7, slowly. Pause regularly to thank God for all that he has done for you, and all that he will give to you.

~ Notes and Prayers ~

Day
62

Grace Alone, Faith Alone

Ephesians 2 v 8-10

We were dead in sins. God made us alive with Christ. So Paul now underlines both what we are saved by and what we are saved for.

Saved By...

Read Ephesians 2 v 8-9

What are we saved "by" and "through" (v 8)?

Where does faith come from (v 9)?

Salvation is not "by works." Why does that mean "no one can boast" (v 9)?

Salvation is not a reward. It is always a gift. We were not saved, and are not kept saved, by our good works of service, but by Christ's good works of service. This is what the Bible means by "grace": the undeserved kindness of God in giving us what we don't have in ourselves or deserve to receive from him—the life and righteousness of Christ. Grace is *God's Righteousness At Christ's Expense.*

This changes how we see ourselves, and others. Salvation by grace, through the God-given gift of faith, means we can never be cocky before God, arrogant towards unbelievers or competitive with other Christians.

Saved For...

Read Ephesians 2 v 10

What have we been "created in Christ Jesus" to do?

Why are even these a gift from God?

Why does it make all the difference that verse 10 comes after verses 8-9, and not before?

We are not saved by good works. But we are saved for good works. We've been recreated by God's Spirit through faith in Christ because of a reason and for a purpose. The reason was God's grace expressed in Christ's life of good works unto death for us. The purpose is the good works prepared for us to do in gratitude to him.

Understanding this distinction is crucial. To know you are saved completely by God's grace in Christ liberates you from the pride of imagining you can save yourself, and from the terror of realizing that you can't. And to know that you've been saved for good works prepared by God liberates you from a lazy and loveless disengagement from the needs of the world, and also from ever feeling insignificant or useless.

Apply

Are you in any danger of thinking your own goodness changes your status before God? What would change if you simply enjoyed being saved by grace?

How could verse 10 transform a mundane, boring or thankless task in your day today?

How would you use verses 1-10 to explain the gospel to a non-Christian friend in one minute?

Pray

Choose one verse from verses 1-10, memorize it, and use it to praise God by recalling it to your mind regularly today.

~ Notes and Prayers ~

Day 63

You Once Were Far Away

Ephesians 2 v 11-13

There's an endless cycle of political and military conflict around the world... suspicion and segregation in our cities... and tensions and hurt in our offices and homes.

Could our species ever stop fighting and find lasting peace? Yes, says Paul, as he turns from how we can be reconciled to God (2 v 1-10) to how we can be reconciled to each other (v 11-22). Again, the structure shows how hopeless the situation is without Christ, and how God has transformed everything through Christ.

You Were...

Read Ephesians 2 v 11-12

Who is Paul addressing (v 11)?

Circumcision of Jewish boys was symbolic of being cut free from sin and belonging to the people of God (Genesis 17 v 1-14). But this sign had become for Jews a source of pride in themselves and scorn toward Gentiles, even though circumcision itself was merely external: "done in the body by human hands." Unaccompanied by interior cutting free from sin, it was meaningless.

Nevertheless, at least the Jews knew about God from his law.

What was the position of the Gentiles (v 12)?

Read Genesis 12 v 1-3; Exodus 19 v 5-6; Numbers 25 v 10-13; 2 Samuel 7 v 11-16; Jeremiah 31 v 31-34.

Why was it wonderful to be part of "the covenants of the promise"?

"Without hope and without God" is a good summary of the Gentile position—non-Jews had no share in the exciting promises of a great, coming King; had no right to citizenship in the people of God; and were strangers to blessings. Without Christ, the Ephesian Gentiles were (and Gentiles today are) without hope for eternity and without God in this world.

Those of us who have grown up in Western culture tend to imagine ourselves as entitled to all privileges; we are very aware that we have "rights." But Paul has pointed out that Gentiles have no rights to any blessings from God. He says this not to humiliate us, but so that we can appreciate the "But now"—so that we can understand how generously we have been blessed in Christ.

But Now in Christ...

Read Ephesians 2 v 13

Why is the "But" such good news?

What difference has Jesus' blood made?

Look back at verse 12. The "But" in v 13 signals that the reverse of all these facts about Gentiles is now true for those who are in Christ.

So what is our status now?

Pray

Use verses 1-3 and 12 to reflect on what your position would be if you had not been gifted faith in Christ. Let this prompt you to praise God for his overwhelming grace to you.

~ Notes and Prayers ~

Day 64

Access For All

Ephesians 2 v 14-18

In Christ Jesus you once who were far away have been brought near" (v 13). And so now the peace and access that all of us need are on offer to us all.

Read Ephesians 2 v 14-18

Peace on Earth

Where is "peace" to be found (v 14)?

Christ has united the two most deeply separated categories of humanity in world history: Jews and Gentiles. The "dividing wall of hostility" was the law of Moses, which Jewish religious leaders had turned from being a sign to the world of the goodness of God into a barrier excluding the world from God's good government. Christ has dismantled it by fulfilling all the terms of the law in his life, and in his death exhausting its condemnation of Jew and Gentile.

So Christ is "our peace" (v 14). Deep inner peace, and lasting reconciliation between people and peoples, is only to be found where there is spiritual dependence upon Christ. The peace of Christ is not just a negotiated absence of conflict. It's the positive harmony empowered within us by the Spirit of the divine Prince of Peace.

How Christ Brought Peace

What was Christ's "purpose" (v 15-16)?

The word "reconciled" is literally "super-reconciled" (*apokatallaze*). Whoever we are, whatever we've done, we can be saved; but it can only ever be on the same basis as everyone else—the death of Christ. It is this common dependence and shared super-reconciliation that brings us together in our churches, whatever our background.

Read Isaiah 52 v 7

How is Jesus the fulfillment of this prophecy, does Ephesians 2 v 14-18 say?

"Peace" was the great declaration, promise and assurance with which the risen Jesus repeatedly greeted his followers (John 20 v 19, 21, 26). And peace, through the cross, is now on offer to everyone. Jesus held it out to "you who were far away" (the Gentiles—Ephesians 2 v 17) and to "those who were near" (the Jews). He still does.

What do both Gentile and Jew Christians now enjoy (v 18)?

Our access is now not to a temple building in Jerusalem, but to the throne room of heaven! And from our reconciliation as sinners to our heavenly Father comes the spiritual power for reconciliation within our churches.

Apply

Are there aspects of your background—nationality, ethnicity, social class, education—that you use as a barrier to divide yourself from other Christians (perhaps subconsciously), because you overvalue these things as being intrinsic to your identity?

How do these verses challenge your behavior, and liberate you from it?

Is there another Christian who has hurt you deeply? How does looking at what Jesus did on the cross empower you to forgive them? How could you seek to pursue reconciliation with them?

~ Notes and Prayers ~

Day
65

Your Church is Amazing

Ephesians 2 v 19-22

Paul now teaches us how to see our local church, by telling us how God views it. And it is spectacular!

Welcomed

Read Ephesians 2 v 19

How are "you" (the Ephesian Gentile Christians) described here? How has their status change from their natural state back in verse 12?

We're not spiritual illegal immigrants. We're full citizens of heaven, enjoying an eternal freedom to remain, passports stamped with the King's blood. And this means we are no longer primarily Canadian, British, Nigerian, American or Polish... we are Christians. Our homeland is heaven.

We no longer derive our primary identity from our nationality, nor from our earthly family. Some of Jesus' most challenging teaching concerns putting God's heavenly family first (e.g. Matthew 8 v 21-22).

Apply

Do you derive your identity, security and guidance primarily from your nationality... your family... or being part of God's church?

If you are part of a large church, what are you doing (as a church and as an individual) to ensure you still behave like family?

Founded

Read Ephesians 2 v 20

What is a church built on?

Read Matthew 7 v 24-27. The wise man is the man who builds his house on the rock of Christ. And Christ is the ultimate wise man, building his own house—the church—on the rock of himself.

What does this mean for our local churches? First, the foundation is finished; it is Christ, it has already been laid, and there is no other foundation to build a church upon. Second, it is sufficient. It doesn't need improving or adapting, or adding to.

Constructed

Read Ephesians 3 v 21-22

What is the church (v 21)?

What is your part in it (v 22)?

Every church is an amazing wonder of the modern world. Your church is God's home, his dwelling-place on earth; his palace, where he governs us; and his temple, where we celebrate the finished sacrifice of Jesus. Your church is a foretaste of heaven—the only "local building" that will last forever.

Pray

Thank God for your church. Ask for grace to grow in excitement and gratitude that you have been built together on the cornerstone of his Son—and for wisdom to discern if you are in any danger of changing or adapting that foundation.

~ Notes and Prayers ~

Day 66

The Mysterious Strategy

Ephesians 3 v 1-3

Many people love a good mystery. And the only thing more satisfying than the mystery is knowing how that mystery is solved!

In 3 v 1-13, Paul explains that there had been a perplexing mystery troubling Israel for centuries, concerning God's salvation plan—a mystery now solved in the most astonishing fashion, and displayed to the heavenly realms in order for God's wisdom to be admired. This passage is critical for understanding the apostle Paul's ministry.

Paul's Location

Read Ephesians 3 v 1

What is Paul as he writes? Why?

Think back over the first two chapters.

What does Paul's mood appear to be (1 v 3, 15-16)?

Why is this amazing, given where Paul is as he writes (3 v 1)?

Paul begins, "For this reason" because he is about to explain again what he prays for the Ephesians (v 14). But then he realizes that he must break off to explain what he means in saying he is a prisoner for their sake—he needs to explain his own role in God's plan to save Gentiles.

⊙ Apply

Paul's joy lies not in his circumstances, but in his (and the Ephesian Christians') salvation. He praises God joyfully rather than bemoaning his imprisonment.

Think about the circumstances in your life you would like to change. What would it look like for you to follow Paul's example here?

God's Strategy

Read Ephesians 3 v 2-3

What does Paul think the Ephesians must have "heard about"?

"Administration" can also be translated "strategy."

How does verse 3 clarify what he is talking about in verse 2?

How does verse 2 explain verse 1—why Paul is a prisoner? Because the way God made his grace available to Gentiles was offensive. The "strategy" involved salvation being offered, without any obligation to become Jewish, through a man executed at the request of the Jewish authorities.

So how did Paul learn "the mystery"—the surprising strategy of God (v 3)?

Paul underlines that his gospel—the solution to the "mystery"—came by revelation, not invention, as he had already "written briefly" (he probably means 1 v 1, 9-10).

⊙ Pray

Give thanks that you live in a time when the "mystery" of God's gospel strategy has been revealed. Give thanks that it has been revealed by him, not dreamed up by men, so that you can have absolute confidence in it.

~ Notes and Prayers ~

Day 67

The Mystery Revealed

Ephesians 3 v 4-9

God's strategy to show his grace had been a mystery. Paul knew the solution. And in these next few verses, he shares it with us.

Insight

Read Ephesians 3 v 4-5

What is Paul offering his readers (v 4)?

Verse 5 is a little confusing. Paul says in Romans that the gospel was "promised beforehand through God's prophets in the Holy Scriptures" (Romans 1 v 2)—here he says it wasn't previously known. But the promise and the strategy are different things. God's gospel promise to bless all nations had been known since Abraham (Genesis 12 v 1-3). What was completely unknown and inaccessible to "other generations" was not God's plan to save all nations but how God could accomplish such a great plan. Now, Paul says, this mystery has finally been revealed to the apostles, including himself. Paul's gospel was not a new gospel, but the ancient gospel revealed and clarified. So... what is the substance of this mystery revealed to the apostles?

Revealed

Read Ephesians 3 v 6

What is the mystery?

We could easily miss how shocking this was. It was never a surprise that Gentiles could join the people of God, through submission to the law of Moses. But Paul is proclaiming that Gentiles can be included among God's saved people without becoming Jewish, but through faith in the gospel of Jesus Christ—and that law-observing Jews also need to put their faith in Christ.

The gospel "was not made known to people in other generations as it has now been revealed..." (v 5). Have you realized that you are in a more privileged position than the Israelites who heard God at Mt. Sinai, or even than the Old Testament prophets?

What three marvelous privileges does faith in the gospel bring, does Paul say?

In the original, "with Israel" does not appear. Our privilege is not just to join old Israel, but to join with Jews in one completely new people in Christ. We are heirs of all that is promised. *Read Revelation 22 v 1-5*. This is what we will share together!

The Preacher

What had Paul become (Ephesians 3 v 7)?

Why was this remarkable (beginning of verse 8)?

What was Paul's role (v 8-9)?

Literally, "servant" is "slave." Paul is not supporting slavery here—then, as now, slavery was a disgusting exploitation of people who were each incredibly precious to God. But it's only when we grasp the horror of slavery that we begin to feel the wonder of Paul's self-description in verse 7. He is a man at God's command. And he is amazed that he would be permitted to be—his view of himself in verse 8 is not false modesty, but comes from his profound consciousness of his previous sin, seen most terribly in his persecution of Christ's church. *Read Acts 7 v 54 – 8 v 1; 9 v 1-16.*

Apply

We will never grasp the wonder of the gospel until we grasp the horror of our rebellion against Christ. And we will never know the joy of serving (or "slaving for") the King until we realize what an undeserved privilege it is.

Do you accept your own sinfulness, especially before you were given faith in Christ... or do you tend to belittle or excuse it?

Do you realize that it is only by "the working of [God's] power" that you know God's grace?

What difference does answering "yes" to these questions make to your view of yourself and your service of the gospel?

~ Notes and Prayers ~

Day 68

God's Trophy Cabinet

Ephesians 3 v 10-13

What is God's purpose in calling the apostles to preach the revealed mystery of the gospel of Christ crucified? The answer is simply breathtaking.

God's Intent

Read Ephesians 3 v 10-11

What did God intend to make known (v 10)?

What did he intend that to be made known "through" (v 10)? How does this happen (remember v 6)?

The "manifold wisdom" of God is the complex brilliance of his salvation plan. And its brilliance is displayed... whenever your church meets together! Every local church is God's trophy cabinet.

Who is God's manifold wisdom made known to (v 10)?

How does 6 v 12 enable us to know who exactly Paul is talking about here?

In other words, every local-church gathering anywhere in the world is like one of those champions' celebrations in an open-top bus: but instead of a football team celebrating a temporary sporting victory in a stadium, a church gathering under Christ is a celebration and declaration of God's eternal spiritual victory over Satan, sin and death at the cross.

Paul's Sufferings

Read Ephesians 3 v 12-13

How is verse 12 in many ways a summary of all Paul has said since the beginning of chapter 2?

What does Paul urge the Ephesians not to do (v 13)? What reason does he give?

How should this affect the way we react when we hear of Christians suffering for our faith (including those nearest and dearest to us)?

There's no need to be discouraged by hostility to our faith. It is not a sign that something has gone wrong—it is all part of God's plan. The news is out—the mystery has been solved, the news has gone viral: Christ is building his church from every nation on earth, each local gathering celebrating and showcasing his sparkling wisdom and amazing grace in the spiritual realms, even amid persecution.

⊙ Apply

Your church is a trophy cabinet of God's grace and wisdom. How will this affect your attitude toward going to church next Sunday?

⊙ Pray

Ask the Lord for grace to see suffering for him and his people not as something to be avoided or discouraged by, but as something to be borne joyfully and confidently.

~ Notes and Prayers ~

Day 69

Not How but Who

Ephesians 3 v 14-15

I seriously doubt whether many of us have realized quite how much Jesus Christ loves us. Let's invite Paul to explain over the next seven verses as he shares another prayer.

Read Ephesians 3 v 14-15

For this Reason

Think back over the first 2½ chapters of Ephesians.

What is the "reason" (v 14) that Paul kneels to pray, do you think?

We could see Paul as having three motivations to pray, by the time he reaches 3 v 14:

1. The wonder of God's plan "to bring unity to all things ... under Christ" (1 v 10), of which his own ministry is a part (3 v 2-13).
2. God's accomplishment of vertical reconciliation between us and himself through Christ (2 v 1-10), and horizontal reconciliation to each other in the church (2 v 11-22).
3. The encouragement Paul had offered in 2 v 22, just before he broke off to explain his ministry—the privilege and responsibility of being part of "a dwelling in which God lives by his Spirit": the church.

⊙ Apply

If you were consciously to remember God's eternal plan (1 v 10), your reconciliation to God and to his family (2 v 1-22), and your place in his church (2 v 22)...

What difference would that make to how you pray each day?

To this Person

Who is Paul conscious that he is praying to (3 v 14)?

What is remarkable about how we can address the One before whom we should rightly "kneel"?

The original Aramaic word Jesus used to address God—*Abba*—is both affectionate and respectful (there is no direct equivalent in English). What fuels us to pray is not technique but theology—understanding not how to pray, but to whom we pray. We have "adoption to sonship" (1 v 5)—so we are entitled to speak to the Almighty as "Father." Our heavenly Father loves us passionately and perfectly; he always knows what's best for us, is always patient and kind, and is always able to provide what we need. He's generous and wise, firm in discipline but quick to forgive, and never breaks a promise.

Notice that the Father provides and enables "family" (3 v 15), which reflects the "family" of the Trinity in which he is Father. Human families are not an accident of social evolution to be dispensed or tinkered with. They are God-given reflections (albeit imperfect ones) of the family of our trinitarian God.

⊙ Pray

Enjoy speaking to God affectionately yet respectfully as your "Father."

~ Notes and Prayers ~

Day

70

Power to be a Home

Ephesians 3 v 16-17a

What is it that Paul asks the Father to give? Three times he mentions "power" (v 16, 18, 20). Not power for wealth or for healing, but for two more wonderful things.

Read Ephesians 3 v 16-17a

Where the Power Works

Who gives power, and where does this power go to work (v 16)?

What can this power do (v 17a)?

Notice that the working of God's power will not be to give us an obvious or visible strength to be paraded around—it is the invisible heart-level power of spiritual conviction, created by God's Spirit. By heart, Paul means the center of our affections, decisions and behavior.

That is where he is praying that God, through his Spirit, who lives in us from the moment we believe the gospel of Christ (1 v 13-14), would be at work. The ministry of the Spirit is to be a floodlight, drawing attention to the magnificence of Jesus, resulting in people and churches in whom Jesus is continually glorified and loved, and people and churches who are full of the Holy Spirit.

What the Power Does

The word "dwell" (3 v 17a) doesn't mean just to arrive, but to settle down—to "make yourself at home."

How does this help us understand what Paul is specifically praying for here?

When someone comes for a short visit, they usually just leave their stuff in their travel bags and try not to disturb the room. But when someone moves into a new home permanently, they change the wallpaper, paint the ceiling, replace the carpet and throw out the old furniture. When the Spirit of Christ moves into a person, he gradually redecorates everywhere. He makes changes in us; and we work together with him to make those changes. As we do so, Christ will be more "at home" in our lives.

We are now a home address for Jesus. That won't always be easy—he loves us too much to do nothing about our sin. He will gently and gradually but radically be transforming our interior—because he loves us.

Apply

How have you experienced the Spirit's power renovating your heart as a home fit for Christ? (If you cannot think of anything, ask another Christian who knows you well. If you still cannot point to anything, then challenge yourself as to whether you are really living with faith in Christ as Lord and committed to living under his rule.)

Which area of your emotions, thoughts or actions is the Spirit inviting you to work on changing, by his power?

Pray

How have these verses encouraged you to pray, and helped you to know what to pray for?

Spend time kneeling before your Father now.

~ Notes and Prayers ~

Day
71

Power to Appreciate

Ephesians 3 v 17b-21

Paul has prayed his friends will have power to change, so that Christ would be "at home" in them. Now he prays they will have power to appreciate...

The Foundation

Read Ephesians 3 v 17b-19

What does Paul pray the Ephesians would be "being" (v 17b)? Read 2 v 4-5 and 5 v 1-2. What is the "love" that we need to be planted in and founded upon?

Four Dimensions

What is it that Paul is praying that God's power would do (3 v 18)?

In verse 18, Paul is using dimensions which are remarkably appropriate to the major themes of this letter concerning God's grace:

- "Wide" illustrates his *accepting* love. *Read 2 v 17*. If you are trusting Christ, there is nothing you have done or could ever do that would put you outside his embrace. And there is no one you know that he would turn away from his embrace, if they come to him in faith.
- "Long" illustrates his *lasting* love. God's love for us began before creation—*read 1 v 4-5*. However badly and however often we disappoint him, he will never let us go. He has committed himself to love us from eternity past for eternity everlasting.

- "High" illustrates his *exalting* love. *Read 2 v 6-7.* We are not only saved from hell; we are lifted high into heaven. We need to grasp how high is the love of Christ, how much he has in store for us in eternity, and how exalted and privileged we shall be forever in the new creation.
- "Deep" illustrates his *sacrificial* love. *Read 1 v 7-8.* Christ experienced the spiritual trauma of suffering in his own soul the hell that all his people deserve. And he did it out of personal love for you. His is an incredibly deep love.

Just as we cannot plumb the depths of the ocean, so we will never fully comprehend this love. It "surpasses knowledge" (3 v 19). But just as we can play and swim and dive in the ocean, we can "know" this love. We can personally experience being "filled to the measure" with Christ.

⌄ Apply

Reflect on a time when you struggled as a Christian, or repeatedly gave in to a particular sin. How was that connected with a failure to grasp Christ's love for you?

Wide... long... high... deep... Which aspect of Christ's love particularly thrills you today?

He is Able

Read Ephesians 3 v 20-21

What is God's power able to do (v 20)?

Read 1 v 20-21. If we doubt this, where should we look?

You and I simply cannot imagine all that God is (literally) "super-abundantly" able to do. When we ask for things that will further his plan to bring all things together under Christ—including helping us to become a fitting home for his Spirit and to know the unknowable love of Christ—we need to remember who we're talking to. God is willing and able to do super-abundantly more for us, and in us, than anyone could ever imagine.

⌃ Pray

Speak to the Father now, praying for power to change, and power to grasp. But don't pray only for yourself—Paul prays this for others, and so should we. Bring to mind those fellow Christians you prayed for as we studied Paul's prayer in chapter 1, and pray for God's power to be at work in them in these ways.

~ Notes and Prayers ~

Day
72

Ingredients for Church Growth

Ephesians 4 v 1-3

Paul now turns to the question: How do churches—God's means of declaring his triumphant wisdom to the heavenly realms (3 v 10)—grow?

Three Ingredients

In 4 v 1-16, Paul is outlining three basic ingredients for church growth. These fundamental principles of genuine spiritual growth are the same for every church in every context. Applying them will take time and sacrifice, but this is how God always grows his churches. And the three ingredients, which we will be focusing upon over the next four devotional studies, are unity (v 2-6) in ministry (v 7-12) for maturity (v 12-16).

Your Calling

Read Ephesians 4 v 1-3

What is "the calling you have received" (v 1—see 1 v 4-14)?

What should we do in light of understanding that "calling" (v 1)?

What does this involve (v 2-3)? What does each of these qualities look like in practice?

Notice that the "calling" is not only into Christ, but also into the unity of his church. This is not about unity between churches, but relational unity within churches. And it is important to understand what these qualities are, and are not:

1. Being "humble" (v 2) is not being shy. It means restraining our sense of entitlement to be the focus of other people's care and attention, and committing ourselves to promote others' best interests.
2. Being "gentle" (v 2—literally "meek") is not being weak. It means dealing with other people with kindness rather than roughness, with compassion rather than force, and with encouragement rather than bullying.
3. Being "patient" does not mean to seethe inwardly but not outwardly; it means to be long-suffering of the faults of others and slow in seeking to rebuke them, recognizing that spiritual growth takes time and that we are all work in progress.

If we are humble, gentle and patient, what will we be able to do (end v 2)?

And what will we be able to commit to doing (v 3)?

The Spirit creates a special togetherness within a congregation. We are to do everything we can to promote it, and avoid everything we might do to undermine it.

Apply

Western culture indulges the view that being opinionated, aggressive and ambitious for ourselves and our families is a good thing. But that is the opposite of these qualities—and it strangles the growth of a church, because we end up pulling our church in different directions.

How do you find it easiest to follow the culture, rather than the example of our Christ?

Who do you find it hard to act patiently toward? How can a deep love of the gospel enable you to remain loving toward that person?

~ Notes and Prayers ~

Day

73

Aspects of One-ness

Ephesians 4 v 4-6

Paul now gives us a great motivation to "make every effort to keep the unity of the Spirit" (v 3) in our churches...

Read Ephesians 4 v 4-6

United as One

How many times does Paul use the word "one" here? What point is he making, do you think?

The aspects of "one-ness" that Paul highlights here are not accidental. He is describing the unity that each of the three Persons within the unity of the Godhead creates between Christians in God's church:

- "One Spirit" has called us into the "one "body of the church through the "one hope" of eternal life in the gospel (v 4).
- "One Lord," Jesus, is proclaimed in the one gospel "faith" of Scripture, symbolized in our shared "baptism" (literally "soaking") in the Spirit when were born again, represented by water baptism (v 5).
- "One God and Father" is the origin, ruler and sustaining presence of everything and everyone in the universe (v 6).

Since God is himself a loving unity of Persons who are different but equal, serving each other, every church he gathers under Christ is to be a loving unity of different but equal persons, serving each other. Your church community can reflect your Creator!

Apply

How can you proactively help to maintain unity in your church?

How have verses 1-6 helped motivate you to take this seriously?

Contend, but don't Quarrel

Read Jude v 3-4; 2 Timothy 2 v 23-24

How can a church both "contend" and "not be quarrelsome," do you think?

Why are both vital, in different circumstances?

Churches can be damaged either by being too soft—when we should be courageously contending for the gospel against false teachers—or by being too hard—when we should be more patiently tolerant with our brothers and sisters in Christ. The wisdom to discern the difference comes from being committed to rejoicing in people from a diversity of cultures, backgrounds and languages gathering into the unity of one gospel faith, in relationship with one Father, one Son our Lord, and one Spirit.

Apply

Do you think you, and your church, are more in danger of being too soft or too hard? How can you avoid this pitfall?

Pray

Pray for your church. Thank God for gospel unity, and pray that you would never take it for granted, but rather, bear with one another in love.

~ Notes and Prayers ~

Day 74

Gifted People

Ephesians 4 v 7-13

Having emphasized the importance of unity in the church, Paul now explains the value of diverse ministries among its members. We grow by unity in ministry.

Contributor Culture

Read Ephesians 4 v 7-10

What has every single Christian been given (v 7)? By whom?

Paul is not referring here to salvation, but to the additional grace of gifts of ministry. These abilities are not given for our personal satisfaction or reputation, but to enrich the life and service of others in our church. They are not abilities, in fact, so much as ministries. And since it's Christ who gives the gifts, there's no point in feeling envious of someone else's gift or proud of our own. We're approved of by God for our godliness, not our giftedness.

In verse 8, Paul looks back to Psalm 68, a song celebrating the victory of God in rescuing Israel from Egypt and then giving his redeemed people back to the world. Paul recognizes that this psalm looked forward to the victory of Christ in ascending to heaven (Ephesians 4 v 10) after descending into the world to die for us (v 9)—and in then giving us all back as gifts to his churches.

We don't just have God's gifts. We *are* God's gifts to his church. We are not meant to be consumers but contributors!

⊙ Apply

Do you see your "abilities" as things that you are good at, to be enjoyed for yourself... or as gifts from Christ, to be used for his people?

Do you find it easy to view church as a "consumer"? In what way? How do these verses challenge that attitude?

A Team Game

Read Ephesians 4 v 11-13

Who has been given to churches (v 11)?

By "prophets" I think Paul is referring here to the first-century prophets (as in 2 v 20) who taught and preserved the faith, alongside the foundational "apostles," until the New Testament was completed.

Why did Jesus gift people in the ways described in 3 v 11 (v 12)?

What is the aim of all these "works of service" (v 12-13)?

"Service" (v 12) can also be translated "ministry" or "worship." We are all to be equipped by our Bible-teachers for our particular ministries so that we would become more united and more grown-up in our understanding of our faith and in our knowledge of our Savior (v 13). This is how your church will grow—it is a team game, and you are on the team.

⊙ Apply

Are you praying for the evangelists, pastors and teachers in your church?

Are you allowing them to equip you to use your gifts to serve your church? How?

~ Notes and Prayers ~

Day 75

Each Part Does its Work

Ephesians 4 v 14-16

Christian growth is all about "attaining to the whole measure ... of Christ" (v 13)—growing to be more like Jesus. And that is what protects and helps our churches.

No Longer Infants

Read Ephesians 4 v 14

What danger does Paul picture here?

Why are unity, knowledge and Christ-likeness (v 13) protections against being blown about like this?

We need to grow up! We mustn't be like children going through successive crazes, or like boats drifting off into dangerous waters. This is a danger for all churches—be it the latest experiential fad, or church-growth strategy, or (in more theologically conservative churches) an arrogant and prayerless intellectualism or ungenerous materialism.

Have you ever witnessed being "tossed back and forth," either in your own life or those around you? How might greater unity and knowledge have prevented it?

Having read the paragraph above the previous question, what would you say is the greatest danger for your own life, and your church as a whole?

And, not Or

Read Ephesians 4 v 15-16

What must we do "instead"?

What happens when a church forgets about "truth"? Or "love"?

What is the positive result of "speaking the truth in love"?

We need biblical conversations with each other. They are a form of Bible teaching that helps people mature in Christ-likeness. And the Bible sets forth the truth of God, and it tells us of the love of God. Neither is optional.

Whose job is all this (v 16)?

Church growth is a team game. Your church needs you to get involved and pull your weight. Ephesians 4 v 1-16 teaches us that we need to maintain our unity, contribute our ministry, and grow in our maturity.

Pray

Our church building has a prayer on its wall to help us remember what is expected of us by Christ. You may find it helpful to pray it in commitment to your own church family:

Almighty God our Heavenly Father,

By your grace in Jesus Christ and in the power of your Holy Spirit, please help me to be prayerfully holy and joyfully obedient to your word and so, as a member of my church, in submission to its leadership, to:

- *Believe and proclaim the gospel that Christ is my loving Savior and living Lord;*
- *Attend regularly my Sunday congregation and appropriate mid-week small group;*
- *Contribute my prayer, time and talents to our church life and outreach;*
- *Give sacrificially for the gospel ministry of our church and its mission partners;*

... in the name of Jesus Christ my Lord, Amen.

~ Notes and Prayers ~

Day 76

Your Greatest Gift is your Godliness

Ephesians 4 v 17-19

A church "grows ... as each part does its work" (v 16). What is this "work"? Paul answers not by talking about church programs, but about church godliness. Verse 17 flows directly out of verse 16. And the simple point is this: *The gift you are to your church is far more about being godly than about being able.*

No Longer

Read Ephesians 4 v 17

As Christians, what must we do (v 17)?

It's very easy to live as spiritual chameleons, imitating the non-Christian world—"the Gentiles"—in order to remain camouflaged and safe from criticism or discomfort. Sometimes we do this consciously—more often, and more dangerously, we live without even noticing that we're accommodating secular morality or secular priorities.

Paul says, "Stop." This is not a suggestion or invitation; it's a command. Paul wants to "insist on it in the Lord." But... how do the Gentiles "live"?

What it Looks Like

Read Ephesians 4 v 17-19

What does living "as the Gentiles do" look like in terms of our:

- *minds (end v 17-18a)?*
- *souls (v 18)?*
- *hearts (v 18)?*
- *moral code (v 19)?*
- *sense of satisfaction (v 19)?*

⊙ Apply

How do you see these aspects of living "as the Gentiles do":

- *in non-Christians around you?*
- *in your own life?*

Not Liberty, but a Prison

Here are the progressive stages of sin: stubborn hardening of hearts leads to personal ignorance of God, which leads to darkened spiritual understanding, which in turn leads to evil behavior, which promises much but delivers little, leaving us always wanting "more" (v 19).

This lifestyle is not a path to liberty; it is a prison cell from which people cannot escape unless Jesus breaks in and rescues them.

And for Christians, it is a cell back into which we all too easily crawl. But because we are different now, we find the cell miserable; we see that it does not truly satisfy; and we see that the door is always open, because the blood of Christ has paid not only to set us free but to keep us free to leave.

⊙ Apply

Why is it easier not to view "the Gentiles" as Paul does? How does having a different view to Paul's affect our pursuit of holiness and our desire to evangelize?

When do you find it easiest to live as a chameleon? What would it look like to be Christ-like in that situation instead?

Is there anyone in your church that you need to help out of their "cell"? How will you go about helping them?

~ Notes and Prayers ~

Day
77

Changing your Clothing

Ephesians 4 v 20-24

Paul has told us to stop blending in like chameleons. Now he turns to explaining how we can be distinctively holy. And just as with the Gentile lifestyle, it starts in the mind.

Not what you Learned

Read Ephesians 4 v 20-21

What does a Gentile way of thinking never lead to (v 20)?

Where are we "taught" how to live a holy life (v 21)?

This is the only time in Ephesians that Christ is called Jesus. Generally, Paul wants to emphasize the Lord's enthronement. But here, he wants to remind us that God has taught us by becoming a man, both to live a righteous Christian life for us and to practice what he preached to show us what he meant.

Holiness has been witnessed in the historical revelation of God in the person of Jesus. Truth and salvation are found in Jesus. We read the Bible in order to "learn" Jesus. Being a Christian is not about trusting a formula, but trusting a friend.

Apply

How does this excite and motivate you about reading the Scriptures?

Old Self and New Self

Read Ephesians 4 v 22-24

Learning holiness from Jesus is like changing clothes.

How do we need to learn to "undress" (v 22)?

What does getting "undressed" prepare us to be (v 23)?

Our attitudes and desires can't just be got rid of—they need to be replaced. So for example, we are not simply to aim to stop being envious; we need to aim to think gratefully.

What happens as our minds are renewed (v 24)?

In other words, we are to become more like Jesus. When we first trust in Christ, God clothes us with his righteousness—his perfection. It is as though I have nothing to wear to a wedding, so a friend lends me—gives me, in fact—an expensive suit. I wouldn't want to wear it over my filthy jeans or sweaty T-shirt! To do so would diminish the value of what I was given. I would want to take off my dirty clothes.

Likewise, God doesn't want us to carry on sinning as though nothing has happened. We are saved completely by Christ's holiness—but we are saved for a new life of learning holiness.

Pray

Thank God for showing you in Jesus what a godly life looks like.

Ask God to show you where you need to "take off" aspects of your behavior or character.

Ask him to renew your mind—your attitudes and affections—and speak to him about any desires that you know are un-Christ-like.

Then ask him to work in you by his Spirit to make your renewed attitudes flow outward into Christ-like behavior.

~ Notes and Prayers ~

Day 78

Our New Wardrobe

Ephesians 4 v 25-32

What does Christian clothing look like in practice? Paul now explains this with some practical examples.

Taking off, Putting On

Read Ephesians 4 v 25-32

Work through Paul's list in this passage, answering the following questions without looking down to the notes underneath.

What are we being told to "take off" and/or "put on"?

How will our behavior in this area either undermine our church's unity and its witness to the heavenly realms, or strengthen them?

Fashion Details

Paul is giving us some very practical, real-life ways to take off our old selves, and put on the new selves—to become more like Jesus:

Falsehood and truth (v 25): No more gossip or damning with faint praise; no more exaggeration or lying; no more hypocritical criticism.

Anger and sin (v 26-27): It is sometimes appropriate to be angry—but it must not become self-important righteous indignation. So it is wise to adopt a time limit for grievances—to give up our causes and campaigns by the end of any day, to prevent the growth of grudges and factions that undermine unity.

Stealing and work (v 28): No more "borrowing" things we never return, over-charging clients, avoiding taxes... but working hard not to spend excessively on ourselves but to contribute to the needs of others. We are no longer to use our hands to get, but to give.

What we say (v 29): The word "unwholesome" is literally "rotten"—speech like this needs to be replaced with words that build up—that encourage and strengthen.

The Spirit (v 30): It is possible to "grieve" God. Paul is referring here to the rebellions of Israel on the way to the promised land, which so grieved the Spirit (Isaiah 63 v 10). We're not to grieve God through endless, discontented grumbling or through moral disobedience, as they did.

Malice and kindness (Ephesians 4 v 31-32): We are, step by step, to replace all our malicious instincts toward those who malign us or disappoint us with a little of the grace—the kindness and compassion—that Christ showed, and shows, toward us.

Apply

As you look at these "old self" v "new self" differences, which ones encourage you as you think about your own life? Which challenge you?

Pray

Think of one change you would like to make in each of these areas, in what you stop and/or in what you start.

Then speak to God about each one, asking for his Spirit to be renewing the attitudes of your mind so that you might become more like his Son.

~ Notes and Prayers ~

Day
79

Motivations for Change

Ephesians 4 v 32 – 5 v 2

It is not easy to be conformed to Christ, instead of living as a chameleon, conforming to the world around us. So Paul gives us two great motivations to get "changed."

Just As...

Read Ephesians 4 v 32

When we struggle to be kind, compassionate and forgiving, what do we need to remember?

How do you think remembering the last five words of this verse will empower us to live "new self" lives?

If we remember that "in Christ God forgave you," then when someone repents (however weakly), we can resolve never to bring their sin up again before them, never to bring it up again before other people, never to bring it up again before our own minds, and never to bring it up again before God in our prayers. And until they repent, we can give our desires for revenge over to God, who ensures that justice is done, and ask him for the willingness to show mercy and seek reconciliation.

I remember a dear friend of mine, a missionary called James, being asked if he could forgive the violent men who shot him in the face and raped his wife in front of him. He replied, "I can forgive them because my Father in heaven has forgiven me for so much more."

⊙ Apply

Is there someone you are struggling not to think vengefully about? Someone you are struggling to forgive?

Will remembering that "in Christ God forgave you" enable you to love that person as Christ loves you?

Do you need to speak to someone and pray with them about this issue?

Fragrant Offering

Read Ephesians 5 v 1-2

Who are we to imitate (v 1)?

How does verse 2 show us what this will look like?

God-like love is not a cold, antiseptic absence of immorality—it is a love that is willing to make sacrifices for the salvation and blessing of others. And this love is "fragrant" to God—it pleases him, and testifies to the wisdom of his plans in the spiritual realms. That is quite some motivation!

⊙ Apply

Think about areas where you struggle not to live "as the Gentiles do"? How do these two motivations help you to change? What will change look like?

Memorize "in Christ God forgave you." When will you most need to call this to mind today? How will you ensure that you do?

⊙ Pray

Look back over 4 v 17 – 5 v 2. Thank God for his forgiveness in Christ, and ask him to help you to change and grow in the ways that you know you need to.

~ Notes and Prayers ~

Day
80

Gratitude Where Once was Immorality

Ephesians 5 v 1-8

Because Western culture is firmly in favor of sexual expression without constraint, lowering our standards of sexual purity is going to become increasingly attractive.

The cost of standing against society in this area will be high. Thankfully, we can turn to a great Christian scholar who battled with this kind of culture in his day, and who clarified some simple, timeless principles that spell out the will of God: the apostle Paul.

Not Even a Hint

Read Ephesians 5 v 1-4

What does Paul say are ruled out for any Christian (v 3)? What would each of these look like in real life?

Why is "not ... even a hint" (v 3) particularly challenging?

All these things—sex before or outside marriage, lust and crudeness, and an unrestrained desire for more and more—are serious to God, and so must be taken seriously by us. If we want to be in God's family, we have to be different.

God's family is not just any old family with low standards, but the family of the holy, almighty God—we have to step up! Notice this includes our words as much as our deeds (v 4).

As well as ruling all this out, what does Paul say we should pursue (end v 4)?

Sexual disobedience is usually caused to some degree by the spiritual amnesia of forgetting God's grace, and then feeling sorry for ourselves and entitled to indulge our sinful appetites. So the solution to immorality, impurity and greed is nothing more complicated than thanksgiving.

⊙ Apply

How are you tempted in this area? How would a spirit of thanksgiving help you resist those temptations?

Will you consciously seek to give thanks to God next time you are tempted?

Let No One Deceive

Read Ephesians 5 v 5-8

How does Paul describe someone who habitually lives in unrepentant sexual immorality, licentious impurity or material greed (v 5)?

And what can we be sure of if we live like this (v 5)?

There has always been, and will always be, someone ready to offer an easier and a more acceptable ethic than the Bible's.

So what does Paul warn us of (v 6-7)?

How does the image of verse 8 picture how we are, and must be, different in how we live?

⊙ Pray

Spend time speaking to God in gratitude for all he has given you; and about any ways this study has challenged you or caused you concern for Christians you know.

~ Notes and Prayers ~

Day
81

Live in the Light

Ephesians 5 v 8-20

Paul now moves from the negative to the positive, from what we avoid to what we nurture as we "live as children of light" (v 8).

Light, not Darkness

Read Ephesians 5 v 8-14

What were we, and what are we (v 8)?

What does this mean for how we will now live?

- *verses 8b-9*
- *verse 10*
- *verse 11*

Notice that we don't just live in the light—we *are* light (v 8). We don't just have new surroundings—we are reborn. We are completely different to what we were, and we have a completely different motivation: doing "what pleases the Lord" (v 10), rather than ourselves or others.

Verse 12 does not mean that we must never talk honestly about sin—ours or our society's—but Paul does mean that we need to avoid a culture of talking about sin that normalizes, dignifies and excuses it. We don't belong to the world anymore; we belong to Christ. So in verse 14, Paul refers to Isaiah 60 v 1 to make the point that since Christ has risen from the grave as the light of the world, we must now wake up, see the world and its squalor in his light, and live by his teaching.

⊙ Apply

Is there a way in which you are having something, rather than nothing, to do with a "deed of darkness"? How will you steer well clear of it in future? What action do you need to take?

How does knowing you can live in a way that pleases the Lord motivate you to live as a child of light?

Under the Influence

Read Ephesians 5 v 15-20

What must we therefore do (v 15-17)?

What is one aspect of "the Lord's will" (v 18)?

What "influence" should we be under instead (v 18)?

What are the differing effects of being full of alcohol and of the Spirit (v 18-20)?

Just as we saw in verse 4, the core of Christian faith, and the way we fight immorality, is thankfulness (v 20). Sin is essentially rebellious and complaining ungratefulness; holiness is essentially a life of gratitude for all that God has graciously given us in Christ. The mark of the Spirit is that we sing for joy, prompted by thankfulness, in our hearts as well as with our lips.

⊙ Pray

What is your favorite Christian hymn or song?

Sing it now in your heart (and with your lips if possible!), and use it to praise and thank God.

To whom could you text a line from that hymn today, to build them up?

~ Notes and Prayers ~

Day
82

Godly Marriage, Part One

Ephesians 5 v 21-24

Paul now turns to Christian relationships. In each, he will call Christians to submit or to lead, depending on their role, as all of us submit to Christ.

Read Ephesians 5 v 21-24

The "S" Word

"Submit" means to arrange yourself under someone's authority. Some have suggested verse 21 means we should all submit to each other—which is actually impossible! The best view is that Paul is introducing a new topic of submission *in various relationships:* marriage, family, work. The motive in each is to be "reverence" (fear, or awe) of Christ.

Paul begins with marriage, and the role of wives—his teaching is simple yet challenging, for it is immensely counter-cultural.

A Word to Wives

What are wives to do (v 22)? How do you react to this?

What does a wife who does this provide an illustration of (v 24)? How is this a motivation to obey God's word in v 23?

Qualifications and Benefits

We must make three biblical qualifications:

1. *Submission is always conditional upon obedience to God*—so a wife should not obey her husband if to do so would be to sin.
2. *Submission is not mindless*—it does not mean never offering an opinion or expressing disagreement. But it is, after all the debate, to submit to the husband's leadership (see Jesus' attitude in Gethsemane—Matthew 26 v 39-42).
3. *Submission is not about ability, but order.* It is not that a wife is less competent than her husband—if he has any sense, he will delegate responsibilities to which she is better suited than he.

Christ-like submission has three benefits:

1. *It fosters agreement rather than struggle.* Instead of leaving marriages in confusion that too often becomes a battle between the strength of a man's bicep and the sharpness of a woman's tongue, God has provided for a clear, loving pattern of leadership and submission in a marriage.
2. *Submission is attractive to unbelieving husbands. Read 1 Peter 3 v 1-6.* Many husbands are brought to Christ through the prayers and witness of their wives.
3. *Submission pleases God. Read Ephesians 5 v 10.* Paul is telling us one way wives can please the Lord. When godly submission is hard, or mocked, we can be sure that the Lord Jesus sees and is pleased by it.

⊙ Apply

If you are a wife, when do you find it hardest to submit? Why? How can you use the gospel to enable yourself to submit willingly?

Do you need to speak to a wise Christian about an aspect of your marriage?

If you are married, do you talk to others about your spouse only in positive, loyal ways? Do you need to change anything?

~ Notes and Prayers ~

Day
83

Godly Marriage, Part Two

Ephesians 5 v 25-30

Submitting as a Christian wife is not easy. It may well not come naturally. But the role of a Christian husband is not easy and will not come naturally either.

A Word to Husbands

Read Ephesians 5 v 25

How are husbands to act toward their wives?

Strikingly, the instruction is not to rule or to lead, but to love. Leadership must be characterized by, and flow out of, love. In fact, this command is repeated three times in verses 25-33 (v 25, twice in v 28, v 33). Husbands are being called to a sustained commitment to love their wives sacrificially.

Paul gives two models for a husband's love...

Our Wonderful Christ

Read Ephesians 5 v 25-27

Christ loved his church most supremely as "he gave himself up for her" (v 25).

How did he give himself for his people?

So what is this telling husbands about how to love their wives?

The Christian husband must love his wife even unto death; and until that is necessary, he is to die to what is easiest for him in countless little ways every day. A husband is to provide for his wife, because Christ provides for his church—not just materially but physically, emotionally and spiritually. And if his career, or even his church ministry, is consistently making this impossible, then he should consider changing it for the sake of his wife.

What did Christ achieve through his loving death for his church (v 26-27)?

And this, says Paul, is to be a husband's chief goal for his wife—not primarily her short-term happiness (perhaps hoping for an easier life himself), but her long-term holiness. He needs to be most concerned about how she will "look" on the day when she stands before Christ; and her spiritual condition will be taken into account when he stands before Christ himself.

Your Own Body

Read Ephesians 5 v 28-30

Any sensible person cares for their body—and any good husband will take responsibility for cherishing and caring for his own wife. If a husband does not bother to think about or make a priority of loving his wife in a way she appreciates and benefits from, he is hurting himself as well as her.

⊙ Apply

If you are a husband, how similar or different is the way you treat your wife to the way Jesus treats the church? Do you need to ask forgiveness from God and her for anything? How can you lead in a more Christ-like way?

Are you leading your wife in such a way that she can gladly submit, trusting you truly to have her best spiritual interests at heart in your decisions?

~ Notes and Prayers ~

Day
84

The Greatest Marriage

Ephesians 5 v 29-33

At the end of this passage about marriage, we discover that Paul's deeper focus here is not upon our marital happiness at all!

Gospel Glimpses in Our Marriages

Read Ephesians 5 v 29-33

What is the "profound mystery" (that is, the deep, revealed secret) in verse 32?

Paul clarified this mystery earlier in the letter: that people of every background are being reconciled to God and each other—being brought into the church—through Christ's death, to declare God's triumphant wisdom to the spiritual realms.

What human event is verse 31 referring to?

So here is Paul's point: when two people who may be incredibly different from each other become "one flesh," this is a powerful demonstration in the spiritual realms of the wisdom of God's eternal plan to unite everything under Christ. The power of the gospel to motivate a Christian wife to submissively support her husband, and to motivate a Christian husband to sacrificially love his wife, despite their sins and their differences, provides a powerful witness of God's gospel plan.

Gospel Glimpses in Your Life

If you struggle to understand the nature of Christ's love for you—think of an utterly devoted husband. If you struggle to understand how to please Jesus—think of a beautifully supportive wife.

How does this picture help you to appreciate what you have "in Christ" today?

If you're single, widowed or divorced, don't miss where Paul directs your attention—not so much toward human marriage but toward the marriage of Christ and his church, which every believer is part of. *Read Revelation 19 v 6-9 and 21 v 1-5.*

If you are not married, are you in any danger of so focusing on lacking the picture (human marriage) that you forget about or give up entirely the greater reality (relationship with Christ, as part of his church)?

What would change if you believed the reality is greater than the picture?

If you're painfully aware that your marriage is far from ideal, remember that it can only ever be a shadow of your marriage made in heaven. And remember that when a struggling marriage stays together, it is not a battlefield but a victory parade, demonstrating God's power to keep us together under Christ—a picture of the gospel.

If this is you, how does this motivate you to keep on leading lovingly, or submitting supportively, even when it is very hard?

Apply

A united church needs united marriages.

How has Ephesians 5 v 21-33 caused you:

- *to see marriage differently?*
- *to conduct your marriage differently?*
- *to pray for marriages in your church differently?*

Pray

Spend time praying now for the marriages in your church.

~ Notes and Prayers ~

Day 85

Gospel-Grounded Families

Ephesians 6 v 1-4

God is a family of three—Father, Son and Spirit. And he designed humanity, made in his image, for family life, in our churches and in our homes.

So, having seen the Bible's guidance for marriages, we now consider what Ephesians says about children.

A Word to Children

Read Ephesians 6 v 1-3

The word used for "children" refers to relationship, not age—but the context makes clear that Paul has in mind pre-adult children who are unmarried and living at home.

What are they to do, and why (v 1)?

It's not that children obey because their parents know best (often, they don't!), but because it is a chance to please their Lord. If you're a parent, it's helpful to find opportunities to explain this to your children.

When children obey in this way, what commandment are they fulfilling (v 2)?

"Honor" means serious respect—it could be translated "fear" or "reverence."

So how do adults with parents still alive fulfill this commandment, do you think?

A Word to Fathers

Read Ephesians 6 v 4

Who is Paul addressing here?

This position in the family has particular responsibility to lead the family (and single or neglected mothers will need to fill in for a father's absence).

What are fathers not to do?

What are they to do?

How might we "exasperate" the children God has given us? By severe or relentless discipline... unreasonably harsh demands... inconsistent or unfair rules... constant criticism... insensitivity to a child's weaknesses, fears and needs. I've annoyed my kids most when I've failed to think into their world with empathy, or confused my cultural preferences (tidy room, quieter music) with moral issues. Perhaps the best antidote to exasperating our children is to resolve to enjoy them as precious gifts from God.

"Training" means corrective discipline. It is loving to provide consistent, clear discipline. "Instruction of the Lord" means Bible teaching—parenting in a Christian manner and teaching the Christian faith. This is a great responsibility as well as a wonderful privilege. And it is one that a church needs to help parents with, but cannot replace parents in doing.

Pray

Not all of us have children in our home... but all of us have children in our church. Commit to praying for one or two families each week for the next year—and when you next see the head of that family, ask them how you can pray for them.

~ Notes and Prayers ~

Day
86

Workers and Bosses

Ephesians 6 v 5-9

God is a family, so we're designed for family life. And God is also a worker (just read Genesis 1!)—so he designed us for work.

This means our offices and factories, as well as our church buildings and mission events, are places of worship. So while Paul's words here are addressed to slaves and masters, he clarifies some principles that, despite great differences of social context, remain hugely relevant for our working lives today.

Working for the Boss

Read Ephesians 6 v 5-8

Paul is not supporting slavery. But his priority isn't to stir up a social-reform campaign, but to address slaves in their daily struggles.

And how should slaves (and employees today) treat their bosses (v 5)?

This has three main biblical boundaries. The instructions must not be immoral (see Exodus 1 v 15-21); idolatrous (Daniel 3); or silencing the gospel (Acts 4).

Whose "favor" are we seeking as we obey our boss (Ephesians 6 v 6)?

What is our work doing (v 7)?

We are to work to please God, rather than people. After all, we are working for him ultimately. As workers, we are one part of the way in which our loving Creator provides for the daily needs of the world. We worship God when we do our work for him. And even though an earthly master may not notice or care what we do, or may be biased against us or miserly in how they reward us, our Lord sees everything, and will delight to reward us in heaven (v 8).

Working as the Boss

Read Ephesians 6 v 9

What do bosses need to remember about their own position?

What do bosses need to remember about God?

Masters must treat slaves, and bosses must treat workers, with the same respect, fear and sincerity as they would like to receive from them. This does not mean abdicating leadership, since leadership is an act of service when done for the good of others. But it does mean being fair and thoughtful, seeking the good of those who work for them—just as their "master ... in heaven" did and does and calls them to do—*read Mark 10 v 42-45*. After all, there is no preferential treatment for the rich or powerful in eternity. CEOs and street-sweepers will stand in the same dock on Judgment Day.

⌄ Apply

How are you tempted to be a people-pleaser in the workplace (or anywhere else)? Why is it so appealing?

However you work—in the home, field, factory or office, and as an employee, an employer, or both...

What would change if you remembered that in your work you can always, and should always, be pleasing to your Father?

~ Notes and Prayers ~

Day
87

Take Your Stand

Ephesians 6 v 10-12

"Finally," Paul says (v 10)—because, far from being an afterthought, this passage is the glorious climax to Ephesians. And it is all about spiritual warfare.

Spiritual Warfare Today

For many Western Christians, such talk of struggling with satanic powers sounds suspiciously extreme, even crazy. We need to understand spiritual warfare from a biblical perspective. Here are five key principles:

1. Satan is a real and vicious enemy of God and his people. *Read Revelation 12 v 9, 12; John 8 v 44.*
2. Satan temps us to doubt God's word. *Read Genesis 3 v 1-5.*
3. The Old Testament records how God rescued Israel from bondage to pagan fear of Satan. *Read Zechariah 3.*
4. The New Testament records how Christ came to defeat the devil. *Read Mark 3 v 27; 1 John 3 v 8.*
5. Ephesians (as we'll see) teaches that Christ's conquest of Satan is displayed in his church.

Our Struggle

Read Ephesians 6 v 10-12

How "mighty" is God's "power" (see 1 v 19-21; 3 v 20)?

What will this power strengthen us to do (6 v 11)?

Who is the church's struggle with—and not with (v 12)?

What kinds of mistakes do churches make when they forget:

- *that they are in a struggle?*
- *that the struggle is "not against flesh and blood"?*

Behind troublesome false teachers are serious demonic powers. This helps us avoid both being cruel toward a person who is deceived (they don't realize Satan is misleading them) and being naïve about nice people who teach falsehood (we mustn't underestimate the damage that Satan will do with his lies, which undermine the gospel).

Our Victory

Read Ephesians 1 v 19-23; 2 v 6-7

How do we know that we can "stand" against such powerful spiritual forces?

After the D-Day landings of Allied forces in France on 6th June 1944 during World War II, victory on the Western Front was ensured. But the Allied troops had to keep fighting the Germans until they surrendered on 5th May 1945. In the interim, the battle was fierce, but ultimate victory was not in doubt. Likewise, Christ decisively defeated Satan on the cross, but will not destroy him until he returns in judgment. Until then, our struggle will be fierce, but our victory is not in doubt.

⊙ Apply

Does your view of what spiritual warfare is need to change in any way?

Do you tend to make too much or too little of the devil and his aims and power? What effect does this have on your view of life and your fight against sin?

~ Notes and Prayers ~

Day
88

What to Wear in a Fight

Ephesians 6 v 13-17

We are in a battle. The victory is certain, but the struggle is not over. So what is our strategy for surviving Satan's assaults?

Put it On

Read Ephesians 6 v 13-14

What must we wear?

What will this enable us to do? (Hint: Paul uses the same word three times.)

"The day of evil" speaks of the days in which we now live (the time before Christ comes, when Satan is active); and also of those specific occasions in our lives when Satan is particularly attacking our faith in the gospel that unites us as church. The battleground of spiritual warfare will be everyday life. Our goal is to survive, to hold our ground, to stand firm together in gospel convictions.

Read 2 Samuel 23 v 8-10

How is Eleazar a picture of what we are called to do in Ephesians 6?

Read 1 Peter 5 v 8-9

Notice that spiritual victory is not about being freed from suffering, but maintaining faith in the gospel despite it.

The Armor

So what is the "armor of God" that we are to "put on" (Ephesians 6 v 13)?

Read Ephesians 6 v 14-17

A careful look at this list of "armor" shows that these are not virtuous actions that we are to start doing! Paul is not urging us to be good—rather, they are all ways of describing the impact of the gospel. The full armor of God—which our champion and commander, Jesus, wore into battle with Satan—is simply faith in the gospel, which the devil wants us to abandon. That armor that Jesus "wore" is illustrated here with the compete kit of a heavily-armed Roman foot solider, which Paul amplifies with the prophet Isaiah's description of the Lord as a warrior—*read Isaiah 11 v 5; 29 v 2; 52 v 7; 59 v 17; and Proverbs 30 v 5.*

The fact that Jesus used this armor and was victorious proves that it is effective. To put on the full armor of God is to resist the lies of Satan with our gospel convictions about the person, life, death, resurrection and reign of Jesus Christ.

Re-read Ephesians 6 v 13-17

Can you think of how Jesus wore this armor in his life and death?

What does it look like for us to wear this armor in our lives today?

⊙ Apply

Consider a time recently when you gave in to temptation.

What aspect of gospel truth had you failed to remember and live by—i.e. to "wear"? How can you stand firm next time that temptation comes?

Where will the battle be hardest today, and how will you stand?

~ Notes and Prayers ~

Day 89

Prayer and Proclamation

Ephesians 6 v 18-20

Finally—and as part of the armor Christians must wear—Paul asks for prayer to proclaim. If he needed prayer for this, then we certainly do too!

The "Alls" of Prayer

Read Ephesians 6 v 18

When should we pray?

What should we pray?

For whom should we pray?

We may feel powerless to help God's people around the world, especially those who are suffering persecution for him—but God loves the prayers of those who are moved to pray for his family.

Pray

Obey the command of verse 18 now...

- for some members of your church.
- for believers in places where you know your brothers and sisters are persecuted.

Words to Proclaim

Read Ephesians 6 v 19-20

What prayer does Paul ask for?

By calling himself an "ambassador," what do you think Paul is saying about his relationship to the gospel?

Where has Paul ended up because of being an "ambassador" (v 20)?

It was his message that had brought Paul persecution and imprisonment; so he needed God's help to keep proclaiming it, and to do so "fearlessly." Paul knew that "everyone who wants to live a godly life in Christ Jesus will be persecuted" (2 Timothy 3 v 12). Jesus himself told his followers that, "If they persecuted me, they will persecute you also" (John 15 v 20).

Dietrich Bonhoeffer, the German pastor imprisoned and executed for his opposition to Nazism, wrote from his prison, "Suffering ... is the badge of discipleship. If we refuse to ... submit to suffering and rejection at the hands of men, we forfeit our fellowship with Christ and have ceased to follow him."

So we must all expect to suffer for following Christ. In secular Western cultures, it may mean enduring mockery from our friends, pity from our family and aggression on the doorstep. Elsewhere, it will mean far worse. So we need to pray for ourselves and for each other that we will proclaim Christ, and proclaim him "fearlessly" (Ephesians 6 v 19-20)—and that rejection or even imprisonment will not be seen as a disgrace or a disaster, but as part of being dignified representatives of our persecuted King.

This is all part of spiritual warfare. Satan wants to divide our churches and silence our witness. We need to put on the full armor of God, worn by Christ and now by us—namely, faith in the gospel being expressed in prayer and evangelism.

Apply

When are you most likely to be "fearful" about speaking out about Christ, and therefore remain quiet? Who will you ask to pray for you?

~ Notes and Prayers ~

Day

90

Three Great Blessings

Ephesians 6 v 21-24

Paul now briefly concludes his letter. His farewell words deliberately emphasize the three major blessings of God in Christ that are prominent throughout Ephesians.

The Messenger

Read Ephesians 6 v 21-22

How is Tychicus, with whom Paul is sending his letter, described?

What will he do when he reaches the Ephesians?

Being described in the way that Tychicus is here is surely the highest of accolades for any believer. Indeed, it is the praise we are all to invest our efforts and resources in, that Christ might welcome us into his kingdom with this description of our efforts—*read Matthew 25 v 21, 23*.

The measure of our lives and ministries is not the size of our salary, the number of our grandchildren, the turnover of our business or the size of our church, but whether we have proved faithful in believing and proclaiming the mystery of the gospel, even when it hurts.

The Message

Read Ephesians 6 v 23-24

What three blessings does Paul remind the Ephesians that they enjoy (two in v 23, one in v 24)?

Paul signs off with the result, the content and the origin of God's glorious plan to unite everything under Christ.

The *result* of God's work is that we now enjoy "peace" (v 23)—peace with God and in his church. *Read 2 v 14-17.*

Love (6 v 23) is the *content* of God's plan—a plan that not only reveals how impressive he is, but how compassionate he is; and not just how powerful he is, but how loving. *Read 1 v 4-6; 2 v 4-5; 3 v 17b-19.*

The *origin* of God's gospel is his grace (6 v 24)—his undeserved and extravagant kindness in gathering us into his church to display his wisdom in the spiritual realms, but also to shower us with "incomparable riches" of life with him in eternity. *Read 2 v 6-10.*

In Christ, we have peace with God, because of the love of God, flowing from the grace of God.

What should our response be to all that we have in our Lord Jesus (6 v 24)?

Apply

How has Ephesians given you a greater appreciation of gospel peace, gospel love, and gospel grace?

How has Ephesians equipped you to serve God by serving his church?

What practical change to the way you live has the Spirit been calling you to as you have enjoyed the great truths of this letter?

Pray

Use one (or more) of Paul prayers, or requests for prayer, to prompt your own prayers today—*read 1 v 15-21; 3 v 16-21; 6 v 19-20.*

Then *re-read 1 v 3-14,* and pour out your praise to God.

~ Notes and Prayers ~

EXPLORE
BY THE BOOK

More from the series...

Let four of the great Bible teachers of the Reformation—John Calvin, Martin Luther, Heinrich Bullinger and Thomas Cranmer—teach you the Scriptures, day by day. Edited by Lee Gatiss, this devotional brings the work of these sixteenth-century giants to life in an engaging and accessible way.

“Makes some of the most spiritually penetrating devotional writing of the past accessible to readers today. Don't miss it!”

Tim Keller

“Imagine bringing the great Reformers to your house for personal devotions. This book comes closest to that.”

Michael Horton

Timothy Keller and Sam Allberry take you through three key New Testament sections. Experience the joy of the gospel in Romans, a book that has changed history so many times. Wrestle with the challenging applications of James' letter to the church. And listen to the Lord's teaching the night before he died, as recounted by John.

Join Mark Dever, Senior Pastor of Capitol Hill Baptist Church, Washington DC, and Mike McKinley, Senior Pastor of Sterling Park Baptist Church, Virginia. They will take you through the twists and turns of the life of Ruth, the searing challenges and soaring promises of Jeremiah, and the local-church exhortations of Paul's first letter to the Corinthian church.

www.thegoodbook.com/explorebythebook

EXPLORE

DAILY DEVOTIONAL

Meet the rest of the Explore family. *Explore Quarterly* is a numbered, dated resource that works through the entire Bible every seven years in quarterly publications and features contributions from trusted Bible teachers such as Sam Allberry, Al Mohler, and HB Charles Jr. The *Explore App* brings open-Bible devotionals to your smartphone or tablet, enabling you to choose between dated studies, studies on a specific book, and topical sets.

www.thegoodbook.com/explore

At The Good Book Company, we are dedicated to helping Christians and local churches grow. We believe that God's growth process always starts with hearing clearly what he has said to us through his timeless word—the Bible.

Ever since we opened our doors in 1991, we have been striving to produce resources that honor God in the way the Bible is used. We have grown to become an international provider of user-friendly resources to the Christian community, with believers of all backgrounds and denominations using our Bible studies, books, evangelistic resources, DVD-based courses and training events.

We want to equip ordinary Christians to live for Christ day by day, and churches to grow in their knowledge of God, their love for one another, and the effectiveness of their outreach.

Call us for a discussion of your needs or visit one of our local websites for more information on the resources and services we provide.

Your friends at The Good Book Company

NORTH AMERICA  thegoodbook.com  866 244 2165
UK & EUROPE thegoodbook.co.uk 0333 123 0880
AUSTRALIA thegoodbook.com.au (02) 6100 4211
NEW ZEALAND thegoodbook.co.nz (+64) 3 343 2463

WWW.CHRISTIANITYEXPLORED.ORG
Our partner site is a great place for those exploring the Christian faith, with a clear explanation of the good news, powerful testimonies and answers to difficult questions.